For Graham and James, who grew up with the first edition; for Paul Rocheleau, who contributed his fine architectural photography; and for Mark.

With special thanks to Elaine Rocheleau, Greg Allegretti, A.I.A., David Bagnall, Lisa Marine, and Lisa Reardon.

CONTENTS

Introduction ▸ vii

Time Line ▸ viii

1 GROWING UP ▸ 1

Learn How Nature Grows Above and
   Below the Ground ▸ 4

2 FINDING A JOB ▸ 7

Learn More about the Basic Geometric Shapes ▸ 10

3 LEARNING TO BE AN ARCHITECT ▸ 13

Explore Symmetry ▸ 16

4 A HOME AND STUDIO ▸ 21

Find the Hidden Shapes ▸ 26

5 FAMILY LIFE ▸ 29

Fold a Paper Cup from Basic Geometric Shapes ▸ 34

6 THE PRAIRIE HOUSES ▸ 37

Cook Frank Lloyd Wright's Favorite Breakfast ▸ 44
Make a Miniature Japanese Kite ▸ 45
Discover Patterns Made with Shapes ▸ 48

7 THE ROBIE HOUSE ▸ 51

Read Architectural Plans to Solve a Maze ▸ 55

8 LEAVING OAK PARK ▸ 59

Experiment with Colors ▸ 62
Compare the Design of Houses ▸ 64

9 A NEW BEGINNING ▸ 67

Draw Realistic and Abstract Flowers ▸ 71
Make a Model Textile Block from Plaster ▸ 73

10 MODERN ARCHITECTURE ▸ 77

Design a City ▸ 81

Build a Cantilever and a Model of Fallingwater
  with Graham Crackers ▸ 86

Listen for Sounds Made by Water ▸ 88

Design with Hexagons ▸ 92

11 HOUSES FOR YOUNG PEOPLE ▸ 95

Search for Clues to the History of Old Houses ▸ 98

12 FINAL YEARS ▸ 101

Plan a Spring Festival ▸ 108

Plan a Winter Festival ▸ 112

Work a Crossword Puzzle ▸ 116

Frank Lloyd Wright Houses to Visit ▸ 119

Notes ▸ 121

Glossary ▸ 123

Bibliography ▸ 125

Index ▸ 127

INTRODUCTION

FRANK LLOYD WRIGHT WORKED on his last architectural projects in 1959—more than 50 years ago. A few years after his death, a song written by Paul Simon called "So Long, Frank Lloyd Wright" became very popular. The song's lyrics spoke of missing Frank and the inspiration he offered to everyone, especially the singer, who said that Frank could change one's point of view.

Frank Lloyd Wright lived a long and productive life. He worked on more than 400 architectural projects and was flexible enough to change his own point of view many times over the 70-year span of his career. His work morphed from Victorian Shingle style to Prairie (his own brand of Arts and Crafts) style, to Textile Block (his own brand of Art Deco) style, to Usonian (his own brand of Modernism) style to, in his final years, his very own wildly creative, very geometric, internationally famous Frank Lloyd Wright style. With each change, he incorporated his original idea of basing his architecture on the basic geometric shapes—the circle, square, and triangle—and the inspiration he found in nature.

Frank was only one of a dozen well-known American architects who were working at the same time—from the late 1800s through the mid-1900s. Architects Henry Hobson Richardson, Louis Sullivan, William Le Baron Jenney, Daniel Burnham, Charles and Henry Greene, Walter Gropius, and Ludwig Mies van der Rohe made significant contributions to American architecture. But no one has ever written a popular song about them. Not one of them changed their point of view as many times as Frank Lloyd Wright did. Read the story of his life to answer the question: Why does Frank Lloyd Wright continue to be America's best-known architect?

Frank Lloyd Wright home and studio, Oak Park, Illinois.
Historic American Buildings Survey and Historic American Engineering Record collections/Wikimedia Commons

TIME LINE

1861-1865   The American Civil War is fought over the issue of slavery. Abraham Lincoln was President during the Civil War.

1867   Frank Lloyd Wright is born on June 8 in Richland Center, Wisconsin, to Anna Lloyd Jones and William Carey Wright.

1876   Frank's mother, Anna, attends the Centennial International Exposition in Philadelphia and purchases the Froebel Gifts for her son.

1886   Frank leaves his family home and Madison, Wisconsin, to live and learn about architecture in Chicago.

1887-1888   Frank apprentices to Louis Sullivan. He works on Chicago's Auditorium Theatre and the Transportation Building for the Chicago World Fair of 1893.

1888   Frank marries Catherine Tobin and borrows money from Louis Sullivan to build a home of his own design in Oak Park, Illinois. Frank and Catherine will have six children together.

1892   Frank has a disagreement with Louis Sullivan and is fired. He opens his own architectural practice.

1902   Frank's Prairie style years begin. He is increasingly well known and considered to be a colorful character around Oak Park and Chicago.

1903-1906   Frank makes his mark on American architecture with designs for the Larkin Building in Buffalo, New York; Unity Temple in Oak Park, Illinois; and the Frederick Robie House in Chicago.

1909   Frank leaves his family and spends a year in Europe working on the Wasmuth Portfolio—a printed collection of his architecture. Mamah Cheney lives with him in Europe.

1910   Frank and Mamah move to Spring Green, Wisconsin, to build a home they call Taliesin.

1915 Mamah Cheney is murdered at Taliesin while Frank is in Chicago working on Midway Gardens.

1917 Frank, 50 years old, spends time in California, where he designs the Hollyhock House and several textile block houses in Los Angeles.

1922 Catherine and Frank divorce. Frank marries Miriam Noel, but they soon separate and the marriage ends in divorce.

1928 Frank marries Olgivanna Hinzenberg, with whom he has a daughter.

1935 Frank works on two of his most famous achievements: Fallingwater in Mill Run, Pennsylvania, and the Johnson's Wax Administration Building in Racine, Wisconsin.

1938 Frank Lloyd Wright's picture appears on the cover of *Time* magazine.

1943-1959 Frank begins work on the Guggenheim Museum in New York City.

1946 Following the end of World War II, ranch-style houses with attached garages mushroom across America. The ranch style was initially copied from Frank's Usonian house style.

1949 Frank is awarded the Gold Medal of the American Institute of Architects.

1950s Frank receives honors from all around the world. Although he is in his 80s, he works on projects throughout the United States.

1959 Frank dies at Easter time, on April 9 at age 92. The Guggenheim Museum in New York City opens just six months after his death.

GROWING UP

IN 1866, DAIRY FARMS and small towns dotted the gently rolling hills of southwestern Wisconsin. In the tiny town of Richland Center, Anna Lloyd Jones married William Carey Wright, a widower with three children. The next year a son, Frank Lloyd Wright, was born to Anna and William. The date was June 8, 1867.

William was a man of many occupations. He was a powerful speaker, a minister, a talented musician, and a lawyer. Even so, he had trouble earning enough money to support his new wife and four children. By the time Frank was a toddler, his father had taken a job as the minister of a church in Weymouth, Massachusetts, and moved the family there.

In Massachusetts two more children were born, and the size of the Wright family grew to eight. There were many mouths to feed, and church work did not pay well. William was unhappy. He ignored his family and retreated to what he enjoyed most—music. He often stayed up all night playing and composing music on the piano. Young Frank loved his father's music, but Frank's mother Anna secretly planned that the boy would one day be an architect.

In 1876 the Centennial International Exhibition, a celebration of the 100th birthday of the United States, opened in Philadelphia. Many new inventions were presented at the fair. Some familiar ones are Alexander Graham Bell's telephone, Heinz ketchup, and Hires root beer. About 10 million visitors attended the fair, including Frank's mother. Anna was trained as a schoolteacher and one exhibit especially interested her—

Wisconsin countryside. © Paul Rocheleau

Frank Lloyd Wright as a toddler.
The Frank Lloyd Wright Preservation Trust

an exhibit of the work of educator Friedrich Froebel. Froebel had developed an educational play set of children's blocks called the Froebel Gifts. Anna thought that the blocks would be the perfect gift for nine-year-old Frank. They would teach Frank that the big shapes of buildings can be made from the small parts of his blocks.

Frank loved his new toy. There were many different things in the package his mother gave him. He found polished maple blocks in the geometric shapes of cubes, rectangles, cylinders, pyramids, cones, and spheres. He found brilliantly colored, shiny papers for covering the blocks, and little green spheres and straight sticks for joining the blocks into simple structures. While playing with his blocks he learned that everything is made from basic geometric shapes. The shapes can be hidden within the outer shape of an object, but they are there just the same. Later in his life he said, "The maple-wood blocks . . . are in my fingers to this day."

Learning to Love Music and Nature

When Frank was 10 years old, his father gave up his work as a minister. He moved his family back to Wisconsin and opened a music school in Madison, the state capital. Frank and his younger sisters, Jane and Maginel, shared Mr. Wright's love of music. The family often gathered together in the evenings to sing and play instruments.

The return to Wisconsin brought Anna closer to her family. The Lloyd Jones family had emigrated from Wales in search of farmland and religious freedom. They found both in western Wisconsin. The family, sometimes called the "Almighty Joneses," was a powerful force in the area.

Frank started working on a Lloyd Jones family farm at age 11. The summer work on the farm was so hard that Frank actually counted the days until school began again in the fall. After all, even school was better than working on the farm, where he had to get up at four o'clock in the morning, feed the pigs, milk the cows, weed the garden, and help in the fields. A very tired Frank fell asleep immediately after supper. Twice he tried to run away, but both times his uncles found him and brought him back. The uncles reminded Frank that the Lloyd Jones family had a motto: "adding tired to tired and then adding it again," which meant to Frank that he had to work until he was tired and then work some more. "Work is an adventure that makes strong men and finishes weak ones," they told Frank.

Fortunately there was Sunday, the high point of the week for Frank. On Saturday night he heated water on the wood-burning stove and took a bath in a small tub. On Sunday morning he put away his dusty, dirty farm clothes, took his city clothes out of the closet, and dressed for church.

The large, clannish Lloyd Jones family had built their own church, and Uncle Lloyd Jones was the preacher. When the weather was good the family gathered for a picnic after the service. Frank loved these happy family Sunday festivals. He was free to eat, sing, play, and listen to the stories his father and uncles told.

Life on the farm was not all bad because Frank was close to nature. He loved the low, rolling hills of the Wisconsin **prairie**. He learned the magic of growing things. He saw the colors in nature change from one season to the next. He watched seeds sprout and grow into plants. One day Frank spotted a red-orange tiger lily in a green field. When he became an architect, he signed every drawing with a small red square that always reminded him of the beautiful tiger lily in the green Wisconsin field.

Frank felt surprise and delight when he found the simple shapes of his Froebel blocks hidden in nature. Tiny green spheres appeared when he snapped open a long, smooth peapod. Pulling back the rough husk from an ear of corn exposed the straight rows of square yellow kernels hiding inside. Feathery green carrot tops showed him where he could find plump, orange triangular carrots growing underground.

His respect for the simple beauty of nature grew with every passing year. Frank learned to see patterns in the freshly tilled soil, in the layering of rocks, in the ripples of water, and in the moving clouds. He noticed the structures of the trees, plants, and spiderwebs. He studied shapes repeated in insects and animals. He learned to see that nature hides the basic shapes of the circle, square, and triangle within the outer shape of everything. This was the same lesson he learned from his Froebel blocks, and he never grew tired of it. Later in his life, these lessons would give him the ideas he would use to create his own style of American architecture.

A New Direction

By the end of his fifth summer on the farm, when Frank was 16, everyone treated him as an adult. The hard farm work had given Frank self-confidence and the strength he needed to face the misfortune he found when he returned home. Fewer and fewer students wanted to study music with Mr. Wright, and he had to close his music school. Feeling he was a failure, Mr. Wright left his home and family. Of course, Frank was very angry with his father, but later in his life he could at least be grateful that his father had inspired his love of music.

Frank Lloyd Wright, age eight.
The Frank Lloyd Wright Preservation Trust

LEARN HOW NATURE GROWS ABOVE AND BELOW THE GROUND

When Frank Lloyd Wright was a boy, he learned about nature by watching things grow. You can watch a bean plant grow in a window by following these instructions for growing seeds between two pieces of clear glass. The glass will allow you to see how the plant grows above and below the ground.

Materials

- 2 small pieces of clear glass with smooth edges, or clear plastic
- Small piece of blotter paper (available at art or office supply stores, or use one sheet of an absorbent paper towel folded several times)
- 1 package of bean seeds
- 2 rubber bands
- Small dish
- Water
- Pencil and paper
- Sunny window

Place one piece of glass on a table top and lay the blotter paper on top of it. Put one bean seed on the blotter and cover it with the second piece of glass, making a sandwich of glass, blotter, seed, and glass. Fasten the sandwich together using rubber bands. Place it in a small dish and fill the dish with water.

Use the pencil to draw the bean seed on a piece of paper. You may wish to include the blotter, dish, and outline of the glass or plastic in your drawing. Write the date in one corner.

When you have finished the drawing, put the dish in a warm, dark place. The seed must remain in the dark until the roots develop.

When bean leaves begin to sprout, place the dish in a sunny window. Check the water in the dish every day. Add water when the dish is dry.

Make a second drawing of the seed when it begins to sprout. Make a third drawing of the bean plant when you notice growth. Make sure to write the date in the corner of each drawing.

When the bean has grown into a plant, you may wish to move it outdoors to a pot or plant it in the ground.

Spread your drawings, in the order you drew them, on a table and answer these questions:

➤ How long did it take the seed to sprout?

➤ How long did it take the sprout to grow into a plant?

➤ Did the roots develop before the sprout?

➤ Did you see a pattern or a shape that repeated itself in the leaves of the plant?

➤ Did you see a pattern in the roots?

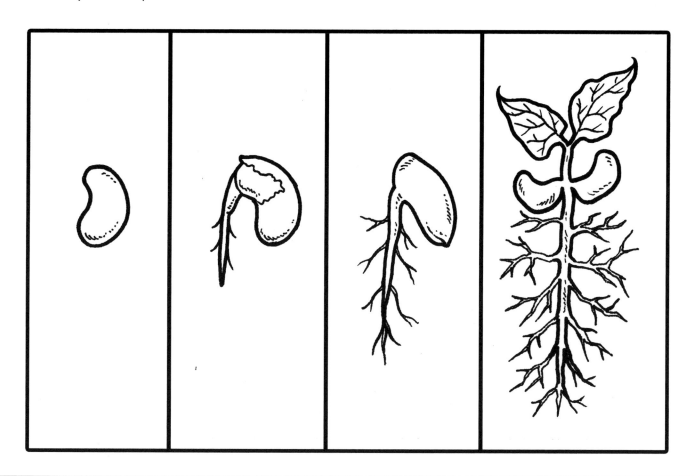

The Wright family was especially short of money after Mr. Wright left, but Mrs. Wright still wanted her son to be an architect. However, when Frank finished high school, there were no architecture schools in the Midwest. Frank's mother saved enough money to send him to the nearby University of Wisconsin for classes in civil engineering—the next best thing to architecture. He found his classes dull but enjoyed working afternoons in his professor's office, where he was able to work on real engineering problems.

The huge dome on the Wisconsin state capitol building was being rebuilt when Frank was a student. One day, while he was watching, the entire dome collapsed, killing most of the workers. The building contractor was responsible. He had given orders to the workmen to fill the supporting columns with inferior materials. Frank was horrified that this mistake killed so many. He vowed to make every one of the buildings he designed strong and safe.

Frank dropped out of school after less than a year. With just seven dollars in his pocket he set out to seek his fortune in Chicago.

The Father of Kindergarten

Friedrich Froebel is best known as the German educator who developed and named the first *kindergarten*, a German word meaning "children's garden." Froebel believed in the importance of free play where children could learn from their own experiences. As part of his work he created an educational toy he called the Froebel Gifts. Froebel used this toy to help children understand **geometry**, color, and mathematics.

Froebel Gifts.
© Kathleen Thorne-Thomsen

2 FINDING A JOB

IT TOOK MANY HOURS to travel from Madison to Chicago in 1886. The long train trip gave Frank a chance to think about the fine buildings he would see. Chicago's architects were taking the lead in developing new architectural ideas.

Tallest Buildings in the World

The tallest office building in the world, designed for the Home Insurance Company by Chicago architect William Le Baron Jenney, was finished in 1885. Frank wanted to learn more about Jenney and his fellow architects Daniel Burnham and Louis Sullivan, who had created a special style of architecture for Chicago. Frank admired these men because they were using new technology—experimenting with a steel skeleton construction that gave their buildings extra strength and made it possible to build them higher than any other buildings in the world.

Because Jenney and Sullivan wanted their buildings to show the steel skeleton construction, they made the outside of their buildings the same shape as the steel skeleton inside. Large windows filled the outside walls and there were few decorations. These Chicago architects felt the height and simplicity of a building was its beauty.

Their buildings were the first skyscrapers, and this new style of American architecture, nicknamed the **Chicago School**, excited Frank. He dreamed of working for one of these great men, and he dreamed of wearing fashionable clothes and seeing everything the city had to offer.

Chicago was a very big city, especially when compared to Madison, Wisconsin.

Chicago History Museum

Then he rode a cable car around the city. Finally, he treated himself to a good meal. After paying for one night's stay at a hotel, he was left with three dollars in his pocket. Frank had been in Chicago only a few hours and already more than half of his money was gone. He was worried, but he did not lose confidence in himself. He made a plan: the next morning he would buy a bunch of bananas and save money by eating only bananas until he found a job.

City of Opportunity

Chicago was growing from a town into a city when it was almost completely destroyed by a gigantic fire in 1871. Because Chicago was the best port on the Great Lakes and the center for the new railroads, the city was rebuilt quickly. There were plenty of opportunities to make money in Chicago and many people became very wealthy. These people needed factories, offices, and homes, and they kept every architecture office busy. There was no better place or time for an energetic young person who dreamed of being an architect to look for a job. However, finding a job takes time, and Frank was short of time because he was short of money.

Finding a job was a discouraging task. Frank was turned down at every architecture office he visited. Sometimes he was asked to come back in a few weeks. That was encouraging, but Frank could not wait that long. He had already grown tired of eating bananas.

Frank was disappointed when he arrived in Chicago. The city of his dreams was a mess of muddy, unpaved, dimly lighted streets. These streets were filled with strange-looking people speaking languages he could not understand. To his country eyes, everything was unfamiliar and was ugly, dirty, and depressing. He wished he were back home.

However, he did not stand around feeling sorry for himself. He had come to Chicago to learn about architecture and he meant to do exactly that. Since there were still a few hours left before bedtime, he set out to see the city sights. First, he spent one dollar to see a ballet at the Chicago Opera House.

Designs That Amazed the World

The Chicago School is the name that describes a number of architects and architectural achievements—including the first skyscraper—in Chicago in the 1880s. The achievements were made possible by new technology and engineering design, primarily the use of steel to frame a multistory or high-rise building. Architects of the Chicago School included Dankmar Adler, Daniel Burnham, William Le Baron Jenney, John Wellborn Root, and Louis Sullivan. Important buildings of the Chicago School are the Auditorium Building, the Chicago Stock Exchange Building, Montauk Block, and the Home Insurance Building, the first building to be completely framed in iron and steel.

Montauk Block building by Chicago School architects Burnham and Root.
Chicago History Museum

LEARN MORE ABOUT THE BASIC GEOMETRIC SHAPES

Everywhere we look we see shapes. There are shapes we find in nature, and there are shapes of things men and women have made.

Shapes are made of lines that enclose space. Some lines are straight and some are curved. Frank Lloyd Wright's set of Froebel blocks contained the most basic shapes that can be made from straight and curved lines: the circle, the triangle, and the square. They are the basic shapes of geometry.

There are two kinds of geometry: plane and solid. The Froebel blocks are examples of the shapes of solid geometry. All the shapes in solid geometry have length, width, and thickness. The shape of each Froebel block can also be shown in plane geometry as a flat shape that has only length and width. For example, a square has length and width. It is a flat shape from plane geometry. A cube is a solid square. Because it has length, width, and thickness, it is a shape from solid geometry. In the same way, a circle is a flat shape from plane geometry, and a sphere is the same shape in solid geometry. A triangle is a flat shape from plane geometry, and a pyramid is the same shape in solid geometry.

Frank Lloyd Wright used the shapes of plane geometry to design decorations and to draw the plans for his buildings. He used the shapes of solid geometry to make his buildings.

The basic shapes of solid geometry are drawn with shading, which allows us to see that each shape has length, width, and thickness. The basic shapes of plane geometry are drawn with lines only.

A circle is a space closed by a curved line that is always the same distance from the center of the circle. The two other basic geometric shapes, the triangle and the square, are called **polygons** in plane geometry. Polygons are many-sided shapes with closed sides made from straight lines. All polygons have at least three sides. The places where two sides of a polygon meet are called angles. Regular polygons have all sides and angles equal.

When we add thickness to the shape of a circle, we call it a sphere. When we add thickness to the shapes of the regular polygons, we call them regular **polyhedrons**. Spheres and polyhedrons are shapes in solid geometry.

Can you name the plane geometry shapes?

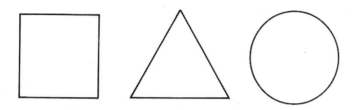

Can you name the solid geometry shapes?

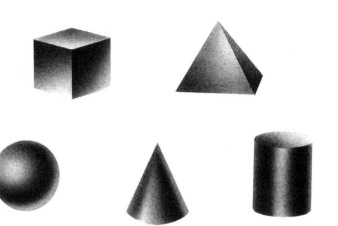

Can you identify the regular polygons? The names end in "gon," and the first part of each name is taken from the Latin word for the number of sides in the polygon.

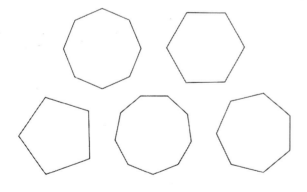

Can you identify the regular polyhedrons? Which plane geometry regular polygons do they match up with?

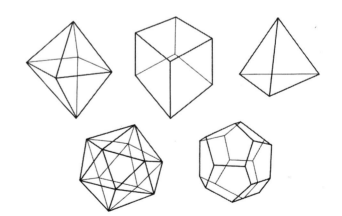

Solid geometric shapes, top row, left to right: cube, pyramid; bottom row, left to right: sphere, cone, cylinder
Regular polygons, top row, left to right: octagon, hexagon; bottom row, left to right: pentagon, nonagon, septagon
Regular polyhedrons, top row, left to right: octahedron, hexahedron or cube, tetrahedron; bottom row, left to right: icosahedron, dodecahedron

Map of Wisconsin showing the location of Chicago, Illinois.
Drawing by Paul Spener Johst. Courtesy of HathiTrust

1 Milwaukee
2 Racine
3 Madison ★
4 Kenosha

Frank, age 20.
The Frank Lloyd Wright Preservation Trust

Finally, he tried the office of architect J. L. Silsbee. He had put off applying there because he knew Silsbee was designing the new All Souls Church where his uncle, Jenkin Lloyd Jones, was the minister. Frank was in a dilemma. He desperately needed a job and telling Silsbee he was the nephew of an important client would help him get one, but he didn't want to get the job just because he was related to the minister. Later Frank would say that he never said a word about his uncle to Silsbee, and Silsbee never guessed who he was. Silsbee was impressed with Frank's courage and self-confidence and hired him for his own merit.

Frank had a job, but he still had money trouble. It would be one week before he was paid, and the money in his pocket would not last long.

LEARNING TO BE AN ARCHITECT

CECIL CORWIN, ANOTHER YOUNG man who worked in Silsbee's office, noticed that Frank looked worried. Cecil guessed he was hungry and treated him to a simple meal of corned beef hash at a nearby restaurant. From that day on, whenever Frank was really hungry, nothing satisfied him like corned beef hash.

A New American Architecture

Frank and Cecil shared an interest in music, books, and architecture. They enjoyed working together and spent their free time walking the streets of Chicago studying in their own outdoor school of architecture. They especially admired the buildings designed by Louis Sullivan, which were simple shapes with large main entrances framed by gigantic stone archways.

Around the archways and at the top of each building was a band of sculptured decoration. The decorations reminded Frank of the plants and flowers he loved on the farm in Wisconsin.

Frank admired Silsbee, but he was soon discouraged by the quality of the work he was doing. He complained to Cecil that they were just making pretty pictures to show Silsbee's clients. The buildings Silsbee constructed never looked like the pictures.

Cecil reminded Frank that architects have to be practical. They need to keep making money, so they build what the clients ask them to.

That's not honest, countered Frank. He was remembering an old Welsh motto his uncles had taught him: *Truth against the world.* Frank felt strongly that people

must do best what they know how to do, not just what they are told to do.

When Frank heard that Adler & Sullivan's office was advertising for a new draftsman, he wanted the job. Sullivan, he thought, was an honest architect. Frank applied for the job, refusing to speak to anyone but Sullivan himself. Sullivan, who never took time to talk to young draftsmen, finally came out to look at the drawings Frank had traced at Silsbee's office. Sullivan was not happy with the work, but he liked the enthusiastic young man and gave him one week to prepare new drawings. After working late into the night for several days, Frank showed Sullivan the new drawings. He was hired.

Frank started work in Sullivan's office with one definite idea about architecture. He thought a new country needed a new style of architecture. Most of the buildings that surrounded him were copies of buildings that had been built in Europe hundreds of years ago. He admired Louis Sullivan because, more than any other architect, Sullivan was creating a new American architecture.

Frank worked hard in the office all day and then stayed after work to share ideas with Sullivan. Often, they talked about William Morris, an Englishman who encouraged artists and architects to work with their hands. Morris believed the shapes found in nature would lead to a new, honest style of architecture. Sullivan explained his **"organic** whole" architecture where the parts of a building fit together in harmony the same way musical notes work together to make beautiful sounds. Sometimes they talked about Henry Hobson Richardson, a Boston architect who influenced Sullivan.

Within a short time, Frank was calling Sullivan his *Liebermeister*, which means "beloved teacher" in German. Soon, Sullivan moved him into a special office right next to his own, and they worked together on Chicago's new Auditorium Theatre and on the Transportation Building for the **1893 Chicago World's Fair**.

Louis Sullivan

Louis Henry Sullivan (1856–1924) was born near Boston, Massachusetts, to immigrant parents. He spent most of his early childhood on his grandparents' farm, where he learned to love the beautiful shapes of nature. As he grew older he walked the streets of Boston studying the architecture of the buildings and neighborhoods. In Boston he was impressed by the work of a young architect named Henry Hobson Richardson.

When Sullivan was just 16 he was admitted to study architecture at the Massachusetts Institute of Technology. After finishing at MIT he moved to Chicago; the city needed architects to design new buildings after the Great Chicago Fire of 1871. In Chicago, Sullivan was restless and anxious to continue his study of architecture. He soon moved to Paris to study at the famous École des Beaux Arts architecture school, the same school Richardson had studied at a few years earlier. In Paris he was exposed to and inspired by decorative Renaissance art. Sullivan returned to Chicago and joined the firm of Dankmar Adler, where he soon became a partner. The firm specialized in large, ornate public buildings. A young aspiring architect named Frank Lloyd Wright worked as a **draftsman** for Sullivan and was deeply influenced by his ideas and designs.

Louis Sullivan.
Crombie Taylor, F.A.I.A.

A building from the White City, the 1893 Chicago World's Fair, designed in the style of the École des Beaux Arts. *Illinois Institute of Technology, Paul V. Galvin Library*

EXPLORE SYMMETRY

Shapes that are exactly the same on either side of a line have **symmetry** and may be called symmetric shapes. In nature, the wings of a butterfly are the same shape on either side of the butterfly's body. Therefore, a butterfly's wings are symmetric. There are many more examples of symmetry found in nature. Many leaves are symmetric. In fact, the human face and body have symmetry. If a line is drawn through the nose down the center of a human face, there will be one eye, one eyebrow, one cheek, and one ear on each side of the line.

If there is symmetry in nature, then there must also be symmetry in basic geometric shapes. A line drawn from the top of a triangle straight to the bottom will divide the triangle into two smaller, equal symmetric triangles. A line drawn anywhere through the center of a circle will divide it into two symmetric half-circles. A line drawn through the center of a square will divide it into two rectangles.

Materials

▶ Heavy paper or cardboard
▶ Pencils
▶ Ruler
▶ Compass
▶ Triangle (optional)
▶ Scissors
▶ Printed graph paper

Draw your own symmetric design using the basic shapes of plane geometry. This will be easier if you first draw the shapes on a piece of heavy paper or cardboard and cut them out. Then you can lay the cutout shapes over the printed graph paper and trace around them. Before you begin, draw a heavy black line down the center of the graph paper. When you are finished, the shapes on either side of the heavy center line must match exactly.

➤ Frank Lloyd Wright learned about symmetry when he worked for Louis Sullivan. If you were to draw a line down the center of the photograph of the entrance to the Merchants National Bank Building, how many examples of symmetry would you find?

Entrance to Merchants National Bank Building.
© Kathleen Thorne-Thomsen

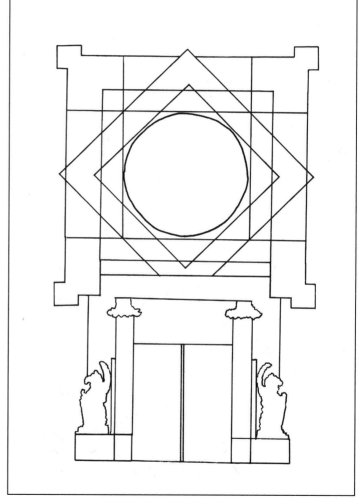

Bottom half of building: windows, doors, lion guards, columns, decorations on top of building. Top half of building: a series of geometric shapes—circle nested in two symmetrical squares, nested in a circle, nested in a square, nested in a circle; small squares in the corners of the largest square; and many decorative shapes taken from nature.

Trinity Church Boston, 1887, Henry Hobson Richardson, architect.

© *Paul Rocheleau*

Henry Hobson Richardson, Creator of a Uniquely American Style

Henry Hobson Richardson (1838–1886) was born in New Orleans, Louisiana, to a wealthy family. Henry was taught at home by hired teachers until he was old enough to attend Harvard University near Boston, Massachusetts. After Harvard, he studied architecture at the famous École des Beaux Arts in Paris. Henry was one of the first Americans to study architecture there. At the École des Beaux Arts he learned to design buildings in the European style, which drew from the **classical styles** of Ancient Greece and Rome. When H. H. (as he was nicknamed) returned to the United States, he was inspired to create a uniquely American architecture based on elements of European design. His architecture—the first American style to be recognized in Europe—was known as Richardsonian Romanesque. Giant curved arches, often made of brick, were a major element of his work. Louis Sullivan and his famous pupil Frank Lloyd Wright often used elements of Richardsonian Romanesque in their work. The three architects were about 20 years apart in age, with Richardson the oldest and Wright the youngest.

Henry Hobson Richardson, self-portrait. Richardson was overweight. How did he portray himself? *Henry Hobson Richardson*

The White City, a Magnificent Fair

The White City during the day.
Illinois Institute of Technology, Paul V. Galvin Library

The 1893 Chicago World's Fair, or "the White City," as it was called, was located on the shore of Lake Michigan just south of downtown Chicago. Chicago architect Daniel Burnham and landscape architect Frederick Law Olmstead worked for more than three years to create the White City. The best architects and designers in the United States, including a handful of women, helped them design buildings in the Beaux Arts style. Thousands of laborers worked night and day to build the White City. Near the end of the project, chief architect Burnham was out of time. He was forced to paint all of the massive Beaux Arts–style buildings in the fairground the same color—pure white. It was an impressive sight to see.

Although most of the White City burned to the ground more than 100 years ago, it is a lasting memory for American architecture. It was the beginning of the City Beautiful movement. Today many of America's beautiful cities have white public buildings that look like the buildings in the White City.

There was also a symbolic meaning for the name White City. Chicago was dark. It had few electric lights and the air and buildings were dirty. Pollution from animal and human waste, garbage, and the gagging smell of the stockyards filled the streets. Many people lived in unhealthy, crowded tenement buildings. Too many city residents died from illnesses caused by drinking impure water. The White City represented a goal to be achieved by other American cities because it was well-lighted, spacious, and clean.

The Beaux Arts–style buildings looked out on shimmering blue lagoons and the waters of Lake Michigan. At night the White City was lit with thousands of Thomas Edison's electric lightbulbs. First-time visitors to the White City were often overcome with emotion. They stood in silence and some had tears in their eyes. It was just that beautiful.

The White City at night.
Illinois Institute of Technology, Paul V. Galvin Library

(right) Frank Lloyd Wright, c. 1888.
(below) Catherine Tobin, c. 1888.
Drawings by Owen Smith

Finding Love

One evening, Frank and Cecil went to a costume party. Frank, who loved dressing up in costumes, dressed as a French army officer carrying a sword and wore a fancy shirt, tight pants, and high boots. Imagining himself to be very handsome, he dashed across the room to greet some friends. On the way, he knocked over a tall, beautiful young girl with red hair. Frank introduced himself as he picked her up. The girl, Catherine Tobin, was amused with him and the two soon became close friends.

When they asked for permission to marry, both families refused. However, Frank and Catherine were determined and they finally won out. Many people at the wedding cried. They cried because they were happy for the couple, but they also thought that they were too young for the responsibilities of marriage. Frank was 21 and Catherine was 18.

4 A HOME AND STUDIO

FRANK WAS HAPPY TO accept the responsibilities of his new life. He had a loving wife and a good job, his mother and sisters lived nearby, and Louis Sullivan had advanced him enough money to build a house on some land he owned in a Chicago suburb named Oak Park. There were a few houses standing on Forest Avenue, but most of the land surrounding the building lot was beautiful open prairie. Frank had designed traditional houses for Sullivan's clients. Now, he had his first chance to design his own new kind of house.

A Home on the Illinois Prairie

Frank looked thoughtfully at the fashionable Victorian-style houses. He thought they were big, ugly, overly decorated boxes. It seemed the recipe for decorating the outside of these **"gingerbread"** houses called for as many different ingredients as possible. It was not uncommon to find brick, stone, plaster, wood siding, decorative ironwork, fancy shingles, and colored glass used on the outside of a single house. These materials mixed together on the surface of the house to create elaborate **porches**, **towers**, **turrets**, **verandas**, balconies, and chimneys.

The big, overdressed box houses stuck out like sore thumbs on the beautiful prairie. Frank wanted his house to remind him of the shapes and colors of nature that he loved on the farm in Wisconsin. He could make this happen if he used building materials that blended together with organic harmony—the same organic harmony he saw in the landscape, where all shapes

(top) A Victorian-style clock was very decorative.

© *Kathleen Thorne-Thomsen*

(bottom) An Arts and Crafts–style clock was simple in design and more harmonious with nature.

Courtesy of Motawi Tileworks

and colors are part of nature's endless and incredible patterns.

He also wanted the house to blend into the long, endless look of the Illinois prairie. At Silsbee's office, he had worked on houses designed in the Shingle style that were harmonious with nature's colors and shapes.

Frank made the outside shape of his Shingle-style house simple, like the geometric shapes of the Froebel blocks. He chose building materials that worked together in harmony like the melodies in the music he loved. He covered the roof and walls with cedar shingles in their natural brown color. He used long brown bricks at the bottom to blend the house with the earth. He placed windows across the front in a band that reminded him of the long look of the prairie.

Frank's organic approach to his house did not end on the outside. He thought the insides of the "gingerbread" houses were as cluttered as the outside. The small boxlike rooms were stuffed with furniture, flashy knickknacks, and every imaginable kind of decoration. Frank wanted his entire house to be harmonious. Both the inside and outside would remind him of the open spaces on the prairie and the beautiful shapes and colors he loved on the farm. He would join his house together in perfect harmony like a musical composition.

At first, the house was small—just six rooms—but Frank made it look bigger. He used wide openings between rooms, and in places he eliminated the walls. He joined the tops of the windows and doors with a continuous band of wood that flowed from one room to another. He designed furniture with simple lines and joined the furniture with the house whenever possible. He built bookshelves, cabinets, tables, benches, and window seats into the house. Walls and ceilings were painted in gold and green—the soft colors found in nature. The house was decorated with wildflowers, leaves, and other objects of simple, natural beauty.

Frank thought his fireplace should provide a warm gathering place for his family. It was to be the heart of his house, and, just as a human heart is located in the center of the chest and keeps the body alive, he located the fireplace in the center of his home to allow warm air to flow through to other parts of the house. His family and friends enjoyed the warmth of the fire when they gathered in the **inglenook**, a small, private place to sit next to the fireplace. As an inspiration to his family, Frank carved one of his favorite family mottoes, "Truth is life," over the mantle. Under this motto was another reminder: "Good friend, around these hearthstones speak no evil word of any creature."

A Growing Family and a New Business

Frank and Catherine were happy in their harmonious, organic home. They were often joined by their mothers, Catherine's father, grandmothers, sisters, aunts, uncles, and cousins. In a short time, they had children of their own. The first three were named Lloyd, John, and Catherine. Since the parents were not much older than the children, it often seemed to the neighbors that the house was filled with all children and no parents.

(left) Inglenook with fireplace.
© Paul Rocheleau

(right) Frank Lloyd Wright
Home, Oak Park, Illinois.
© Paul Rocheleau

Wright family c. 1891, from left
to right: Catherine, baby Lloyd,
Anna Lloyd Jones Wright,
Maginel, and Frank.
*The Frank Lloyd Wright
Preservation Trust*

People who visited Frank and Catherine's house talked about it because it was unusual. People who were afraid of things that seemed strange because they were new and different did not like the house, but those with open minds were drawn to it. Some of them visited Frank at home and asked him for house designs.

At home in Oak Park, Frank began working on architectural projects without telling Sullivan. Eventually, Sullivan found out and was angry. He told Frank he must work only for him. Frank wanted to work on his own projects in his free time and stood his ground.

After working for his *Liebermeister* for less than five years, Frank left and opened his own office. Although he would miss working with Louis Henry Sullivan, it was time for him to leave. Frank had one worry: would clients continue to bring him work now that he was on his own?

Full of dreams, Frank moved into an office space with Cecil Corwin in downtown Chicago. They hoped for big projects like the ones they had worked on for Silsbee and Sullivan, but the big projects did not come and they had to work on smaller projects. In 1893 a businessman named William Winslow asked Frank to design a house. Winslow thought of himself as an amateur architect and could have designed his own house, but he thought Frank would do a better job.

Frank's design for the Winslow House attracted attention. Tile on the sides of the house and strong horizontal bands of brick emphasized the lines of the prairie. Perhaps the most amazing feature of the house was the roof that appeared to float over the house. When the Winslow House was completed, Frank was on his way to success.

Eventually Frank left the office in downtown Chicago and moved back to Oak Park, where he built a drafting room in his original house. But Frank's family kept filling up his work space. In 1898, he solved the problem by building a new studio next to the house. This way, he could have a private work space close to his family. The office had an octagonal (eight-sided) library and a drafting room with a **balcony** that was balanced between the floor and ceiling with a clever system of chains and weights engineered by Frank.

A willow tree stood between the house and the new studio. Frank could not bear to cut down the beautiful tree so he left it in place and built a passageway around it. Many neighbors on Forest Avenue talked about the unusual house with a tree growing up through the roof.

(left) Winslow House, River Forest, Illinois.
© *Paul Rocheleau*

(right) Flower planter outside Frank Lloyd Wright Studio.
© *Donald Hoffman*

Studio drafting room.

© *Paul Rocheleau*

Studio library.

© *Paul Rocheleau*

FIND THE HIDDEN SHAPES

Meet Johnny Mouse, a storybook character drawn by Frank's younger sister Maginel. Maginel was a very talented children's book illustrator. Like Frank, she often used the shapes of the Froebel blocks—the circle, square, and triangle—in her drawings.

The illustrations shown here are from a book called *The Tale of Johnny Mouse.* Look carefully at each illustration and find the shapes of the Froebel blocks. In some cases Maginel wanted the viewer's eye to complete the shape.

On this page, find circles of several sizes, small squares, larger rectangles, and triangles within triangles.

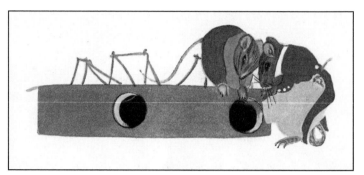

There are many geometric shapes hidden in the illustrations on this page. How many circles, big and small, do you see? Is there a part of a circle? What else do you see?

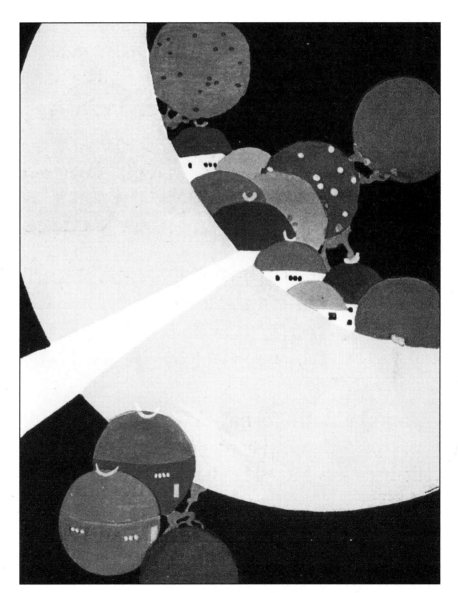

5 FAMILY LIFE

CATHERINE AND FRANK'S HOUSE grew in wonderful ways to make room for three new children, David, Frances, and Robert Llewellyn. The children needed bedrooms, so Frank cut his old upstairs drafting room in half to make a girls' bedroom and a boys' bedroom. To make the small rooms feel bigger, Frank left a big open space at the top of the wall separating them. The open space allowed light and air to travel freely from one room to another. The children were delighted with their new bedrooms, for they soon discovered that pillows, toys, and secret messages could also travel very easily over the wall with no top.

Around the table in the new dining room were chairs with very high backs. When the children sat on the chairs, the backs seemed to reach up past their heads to the ceiling. They felt like Alice in Wonderland in a small private room within a big room.

When guests came for dinner, the children giggled upstairs. They wondered how long it would take the guests to guess the secret of the dining room's lighting. They imagined the surprised look on their faces when they noticed the shadows of tree branches on the dining room table.

The secret to the shadows was a wooden grille and paper that covered an empty space in the ceiling where lightbulbs were hidden. When the lights were turned on, the grille appeared to be flooded with sunlight. Before dinner, the children helped Frank put freshly cut tree branches above the paper.

Enlargement of a drawing by Frank's sister, Maginel Wright, of Catherine Wright and her children.
The Frank Lloyd Wright Preservation Trust

(left) Dining room, Frank Lloyd Wright Home, Oak Park, Illinois.
©Paul Rocheleau

(right) Dining room and playroom grill.
Greg Allegretti, A.I.A.

For the children, the most wonderful new addition was at the top of the house. A stairway and a dark hall with a very low ceiling led to a mysterious doorway with curtains. When they opened the curtains, they found themselves in a gigantic, sunny playroom. The ceiling high above them had another decorative wooden grille. A balcony was their tree house. They could sit on the window seats and imagine that they were looking down on the world from their own fairy-tale castle.

The playroom was the center of family life, where the children played with their toys, Froebel blocks, marbles, dolls, metal soldiers, stuffed animals, and tiddlywinks. Frank played with his toys too. He was known to have filled the room with dozens of colored helium balloons and arranged them in patterns on the ceiling. Catherine taught kindergarten classes to her first three children and neighborhood children in the playroom. On some evenings the family orchestra practiced there: Lloyd played the cello, John played the violin, Catherine sang, David played the flute, Frances played the piano, and baby Llewellyn played the mandolin.

Frank wanted a grand piano in the playroom. He did not want to take up the children's play space with the big instrument, so he devised an unusual solution to the problem. He cut a piano-sized hole in a wall. When the piano was moved into place, the keyboard was on the playroom side of the wall and the rest of the piano hung out over the stairway on the other side of the wall.

During the weeks before Christmas, Catherine and Frank's sister, Maginel, baked cookies. On Christmas Eve, the children hung their stockings on the fireplace. In the morning their playroom was transformed into a fairyland. A huge tree decorated with ornaments, tinsel, and real candles stood in the center of the room. The stockings were stuffed with oranges, nuts, candy, spiced cakes, cookies in the shapes of little men, and surprises wrapped in funny packages.

Some presents, like doll carriages and bicycles, were left unwrapped under the tree, but the best presents of all were in big boxes wrapped in fancy paper and tied with ribbons.

Children's playroom, view of fireplace. © Paul Rocheleau

(top) Catherine Wright, Frank Lloyd Wright's wife.

Their children:
(top row)
(Frank) Lloyd Wright Jr.,
John Lloyd Wright,
Catherine Lloyd Wright.

(bottom row)
David Samuel Wright,
Frances Lloyd Wright,
Robert Llewellyn Wright.

The Frank Lloyd Wright Preservation Trust

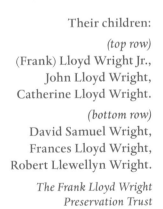

The children would struggle to unwrap the boxes and find smaller boxes wrapped the same way inside. Frank watched with delight as they unwrapped box after box, finding box after box inside. Finally, inside the smallest box was a tiny china doll or a funny mechanical animal.

When Easter arrived, the family gathered budding tree branches and other signs of spring and carried them up to the playroom. Catherine, Maginel, and the little girls purchased silk flowers and ribbons to decorate their straw hats. Everyone in the family had a new Easter outfit to wear to the services at Uncle Jenkin's All Souls Church. Afterward, Catherine and the grandmothers cooked a special feast. The children played games and hunted for colored eggs and baskets full of fuzzy chicks and candy. Easter was a wonderful holiday. It reminded Frank of the Sunday family festivals he loved on the farm in Wisconsin.

Frank spent his Saturdays at auctions looking at antiques. When he brought a treasure home, he would spend hours rearranging the furniture to suit the new addition. Sometimes Catherine wished all of the furniture in the house was either built in or nailed down so Frank would stop moving it around.

A Rising Star

By age 30 Frank was well liked by his Oak Park neighbors and was well known in other parts of the Chicago area too. He wore dashing clothes and found endless ways to knot his handsome neckties. He had a wonderful laugh and a talent for turning tears into laughter. People said the party began when Frank arrived and ended when he left. Whenever he had an opportunity, Frank spoke to groups of people interested in his organic architecture. The publicity helped to make him a very popular architect. Soon he received a tempting offer.

Christmas illustration drawn by Frank's sister Maginel.
Delineator Magazine, December 1912

FOLD A PAPER CUP
FROM BASIC GEOMETRIC SHAPES

Another way to learn to see the hidden shapes within an object is to fold simple shapes with paper. In Japan, ways of making birds, flowers, and animals from folded paper were passed from generation to generation. This playful paper craft is called origami. Origami objects are made from small squares of paper without gluing, cutting, or stapling. Since the shape of all origami folds are the basic geometric shapes of the triangle, square, and rectangle, origami is another way for you to learn to see the hidden shapes within an object. Directions follow for a simple paper cup you can fill with a surprise.

Materials

▸ Multicolored origami paper, approximately 4½ by 4½ inches

▸ Clean worktable

For this project you will need a package of multicolored origami paper. Origami paper is sold in arts and crafts shops, stationery and toy stores, and Asian gift shops. If you cannot find this paper, have one of your parents help you cut plain white squares from any medium-weight paper. If you are cutting your own squares, they must be carefully measured and cut into perfect squares.

1. Begin working with the white side of the paper up. Fold the paper in half along one of the diagonals.

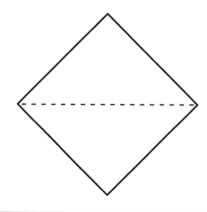

2. Fold point **A** to meet point **B** and crease along the fold.

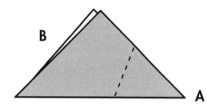

3. Fold point **C** to meet point **D** and crease along the fold.

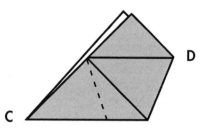

4. There are two flaps of paper at the top of the paper cup. Fold one flap to the outside and crease along the fold.

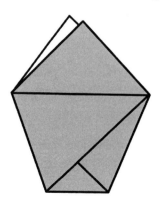

5. Turn the paper over and fold the second flap of paper to the outside. Crease along the fold.

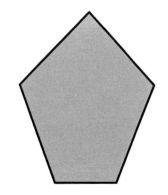

6. You should be holding a small cup shape with an opening in the top. The drawings show the front and back sides of the cup.

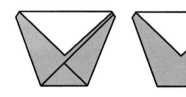

6 THE PRAIRIE HOUSES

AT A PARTY ONE NIGHT in the mid-1890s, the successful Chicago architect Daniel Burnham took Frank aside and made him an amazing offer. Burnham's firm would pay all the expenses for Frank to study architecture in Europe for six years and take his family with him. When Frank finished his studies, he would have an important job waiting for him in Burnham's Chicago office.

Many thoughts raced through Frank's head. Burnham's offer was tempting, and it would mean security for Frank's family, but all of Burnham's buildings were designed in the classical European style. Frank remembered the motto he had been taught by his uncles, "Truth against the world." Frank's truth was the prairie house and an honest new style of American architecture. As long as there were clients for his houses, it was worth giving up security for the truth he found in his own ideas. Frank explained to Burnham why he could not accept the generous offer. Burnham could not understand his reason. He felt his buildings, designed in the classical style, would only grow more popular with the passing years.

Frank's organic prairie houses had special meaning for him. They were a **symbol** of the freedom to move around in America's great open spaces. His houses hugged the earth in unity with nature, and he wanted them to provide more than shelter. He wanted the prairie houses to provide security and happiness to those who lived in them.

Heurtley House, 1902, Oak Park, Frank Lloyd Wright, architect.
© Paul Rocheleau

When Frank designed a prairie house, he remembered the music his father had taught him. The structure in a musical composition is like the structure of a house. When he thought of a house, he thought about music. He saw that harmony and the combinations of several melodies in music were the same as the harmony and combinations of colors and building materials used to make a house. He used the dramatic changes that loud and soft sounds and rhythm made in music to make the spaces in his house more interesting.

What Makes a Prairie House?

Although Frank experimented with each new prairie house, there were several ideas that continued from house to house. Prairie houses did not have attics or basements, which he thought of as

Flatiron Building, 1902, New York, New York, Daniel Burnham, architect.
© Paul Rocheleau

Daniel Burnham's Vision for American Cities

Daniel Burnham (1846–1912) was raised in Chicago in a family with a strong philosophy: a person should strive to be of service to others. After his apprenticeship to Chicago architect William Le Baron Jenney he opened an office with John Wellborn Root. Burnham and Root were the architects of many Chicago School buildings and of the Flatiron Building in New York City. After Root's death, Burnham was the chief architect and planner of the 1893 Chicago World's Fair, or the White City, which was a masterpiece of city planning and a showplace of Beaux Arts–style architecture. The White City would influence the design and planning of American cities for the next century. Although he was strongly criticized for promoting the European Beaux Arts style, especially by Frank Lloyd Wright, Burnham was considered to be the most prominent architect in the United States at the beginning of the 20th century. He is also remembered for his city planning achievements.

storage places for things that should be thrown away. Without an attic, the roof hugged the top of the house and pushed out beyond the walls as though it was reaching down to touch the earth. Without a basement to separate it from the earth, the prairie house appeared to be planted in the ground.

Prairie houses were constructed with simple harmonious building materials. Wood looked like wood, and brick was the color of the clay it was made from. The natural colors of the building materials were never hidden under colored paint. Frank emphasized the long look of the prairie by using strong horizontal lines on the outside of the houses. Bands of horizontal windows looked like ribbons made of glass that had been wrapped around the house. The windows were textured with softly colored, stained glass designs that Frank drew from patterns he found in nature.

The main living areas of a prairie house opened up into one large space. The only divisions between the rooms were one huge fireplace in the center and walls that sometimes did not quite touch the ceiling.

The outside walls of a prairie house reached out beyond the house to the surrounding open spaces. Patios and **terraces** planted with flower gardens, bushes, and trees helped to blend the house with the landscape.

Houses Full of Surprises

In 1902, Oak Park neighbors asked Frank to design a house that was very grand when viewed from

Heurtley House living room.
© Paul Rocheleau

the street. Frank pleased Arthur and Grace Heurtley with a dramatic design. Most other neighborhood houses had front doors in the center of the house. The Heurtleys' front door was off-center and framed by a huge brick arch. The walls of the house were constructed from two different kinds of bricks set in alternating rows. The house look like it was made from ribbons of bricks. Frank repeated the ribbons in long rows of horizontal windows.

Awesome Arches

When Frank designed his prairie houses he was remembering the lessons he had learned from Louis Sullivan and Henry Hobson Richardson. In the Trinity Church Rectory, a minister's home designed by Richardson, the architect framed the entrance with a distinctive arch. The arch was an important element of the Richardsonian Romanesque style. Sullivan used an arch over the entrance of buildings throughout his career. Sullivan's Transportation Building, a project Frank worked on at Adler & Sullivan, is a fine example. Compare the Transportation Building's highly decorative arch with the simple Trinity Church Rectory arch. Is Frank's arch over the doorway to the Heurtley House (page 36) decorative or simple?

Entrance arch, Trinity Church Rectory, 1879–89, Boston, Henry Hobson Richardson, architect.
© Paul Rocheleau

Transportation Building, Chicago World's Fair 1893. Louis Sullivan, architect.
Illinois Institute of Technology, Paul V. Galvin Library

Inside, the house was full of surprises. Frank used the space that would have been an attic to make a soaring living room ceiling. The fireplace shape was an arch. When a fire burned, it looked like the setting sun with rays stretching outward. Lighted glass in the ceiling felt like open sky above. Another surprise was the location of the living room and dining room on the top floor of the house. This space had always been used for bedrooms in traditional American houses.

The same year, another neighbor asked Frank to design a house for his family. This was an opportunity for Frank to try out some of his new ideas. Edwin Cheney and his wife Martha—nicknamed Mamah—did not mind that the house would not exactly fit into a neighborhood of exceptionally large Victorian houses. In contrast to the tall Victorians, Frank designed a house that was simple in design and appeared to be only one story. A low horizontal brick wall partially hid the front of the house from the street. Behind the low wall, the low roof sheltered the house and reached out beyond the walls and below the roofline. The size of the house was another trick-of-the-eye. It looked small from the street but inside it was very roomy. The backyard dropped off down a hill, creating space for a second story.

While working on the Cheney House, Frank and Mamah became close friends. This friendship would create problems in a few years.

Frank had opportunities to design many houses not only in and around Oak Park but also in the greater Chicago area and as far away as Wisconsin, Michigan, and Buffalo, New York.

Cheney House.
Doug Steiner, The Steiner Agency Inc.

Some of the best-known Illinois prairie houses are the Susan Lawrence Dana House, the Ward Willits House, and the Avery Coonley House. In the Coonley house Frank designed a special place for children. The playroom had stained glass windows that taught the children the lesson of the Froebel blocks. Squares, rectangles, and circles all worked together to create a pleasing geometric pattern. Frank even hid a tiny American flag in one of the rectangles as a special surprise.

Challenging New Assignments

Frank's years in Oak Park brought success and recognition. He began getting requests to design buildings other than private homes. In 1904, the Larkin Company of Buffalo, New York—a company with revolutionary ideas—hired an architect who also had revolutionary ideas. Frank was pleased to accept the Larkin challenge. Because he thought of an office building as a part-time home

A Progressive American Company

The Larkin Company was founded in 1875 by John D. Larkin. The original Larkin products were a laundry soap named "Sweet Home" and an oatmeal soap. In a few years the company began to experiment with revolutionary ideas. Larkin representatives sold soap door-to-door, which was unusual in those days. Elbert Hubbard—a member of the Larkin family who would later become famous in his own right—experimented with brand identity and a marketing campaign. These ideas are common today but were unusual in the late 1800s.

Hubbard's ideas worked, and the Larkin Company became very successful. By 1900, when the company was just 25 years old, it was manufacturing packaged foods and other household items as well as pottery, glassware, leather, and furniture. When a new office building was needed, the company hired a revolutionary architect, Frank Lloyd Wright. John D. Larkin was concerned about the well-being of his employees, many of whom were young women. Providing them with a comfortable, pleasant workspace was a request he made of Wright. The building Wright designed was a huge success.

Larkin Building, Buffalo, New York.
Museum of Modern Art, New York

for workers, all of the secretaries in the Larkin Building were grouped together in a large, cheerful open space on the first floor. Private offices for managers were on balconies overlooking them. A giant skylight built into the ceiling flooded the work space with sunlight.

Frank engineered the first complete air-conditioning system to keep the Larkin Building workers comfortable. He also designed the first fireproof metal office furniture for them. Architects all over the world acknowledged the Larkin Building as a great step forward for modern architecture.

Another challenging new assignment was offered to Frank in 1906. Frank's mother's family—the Lloyd Joneses—were members of the Unitarian faith. They believed in the unity of mankind. Frank's uncle Jenkin Lloyd Jones was a well-known Unitarian minister in Chicago. So, it was not surprising that Frank was asked to design a new Unitarian church not far from his home in Oak Park.

Frank persuaded the congregation of the Oak Park Unitarian Church to build one of his unusual designs. Since the congregation had very little money to spend, Frank insisted on using inexpensive concrete for the new church. Concrete had never been used before to construct a large public building because people thought it was ugly. Frank changed the plain gray surface of the concrete to a beautiful texture by mixing small pebbles with the other ingredients—cement, sand, and water.

He designed Unity Temple to look like anything but a traditional church. The roof was flat, there was no steeple, and it was shaped like the

Froebel blocks—two cubes connected with a rectangle. Unlike other churches, Unity Temple was built close to the ground. The congregation could view the sky from inside the sanctuary. Frank felt men and women should reflect on how they behave and how they live their lives on earth when they praise God.

Not all of Frank's work was brand-new construction. One of his wealthy clients, Colonel George Fabyan, rather liked the old farmhouse that came with a large country estate he purchased in Geneva, Illinois. Frank, who grew up in and around Wisconsin farmhouses, may have actually looked forward to remodeling one.

The Fabyans provided Frank with something else he had dreamed about: acres and acres of Illinois prairie to surround his design for the Fabyan Villa.

Frank's managed to hide the front door of the farmhouse, a trick-of-the-eye he would play more and more often.

Unity Temple, Oak Park, Illinois.
© Paul Rocheleau

Fabyan Villa, 1915.
Friends of Fabyan

Unity Temple, interior.
© Paul Rocheleau

COOK FRANK LLOYD WRIGHT'S FAVORITE BREAKFAST

Frank Lloyd Wright liked simple foods. Here is a recipe for a special kind of oatmeal he ate for breakfast every morning. This recipe can be made with regular oatmeal, but steel-cut oats will make the oatmeal chewier.

Steel-cut oats or oatmeal, sometimes called Irish or Scottish oatmeal, is available at health food stores and specialty food shops.

Frank Lloyd Wright's Steel-Cut Oatmeal

Adult supervision required

Ingredients

▸ 2 cups water

▸ 3/8 teaspoon salt

▸ 1/2 cup steel-cut oats

▸ Butter (optional)

▸ Milk or cream (optional)

▸ Brown sugar (optional)

Utensils

▸ Plastic or metal measuring cups

▸ Measuring spoons

▸ Saucepan with cover

▸ Wooden spoon

Measure the water and pour it into a saucepan. Add the salt and bring the water to a boil. Add the oats. Turn down the heat and cook slowly (uncovered) for 20 minutes, stirring occasionally, until most of the water is absorbed. Turn off the flame, cover the saucepan, and leave it on the stove for 5 to 10 minutes. Serve the oatmeal hot. You may wish to add a teaspoon of butter, milk or cream, and brown sugar to your bowl of steel-cut oats.

MAKE A MINIATURE JAPANESE KITE

Frank visited Japan several times during his lifetime. In the early days of the 20th century the only way to travel to Japan was slowly—aboard a giant steamship. Frank made his first trip in 1905. While he was in Japan he became interested in Japanese art, especially Japanese woodblock prints. During his lifetime Frank became an expert on Japanese prints. In fact, he collected and sold them as a side business to his architectural practice.

Designs for Japanese kites are reminiscent of woodblock prints. They are often decorated with characters from Japanese folk stories and with birds, fish, and insects. Kites are popular with Japanese children, who fly them on Japanese Children's Day and at other celebrations. In this activity, you will make and decorate a tiny Japanese kite. You may wish to make kites of your own design using symmetrical shapes from nature.

Materials

▶ A copy of the butterfly kite pattern on page 46, traced or xeroxed from the book

▶ Colored markers

▶ Scissors

▶ Clear tape

▶ Small hole punch

▶ Drinking straw cut into 5-inch length

▶ 2 pieces of thin colored string, 32 inches long each

▶ 6–8 pieces of brightly colored thin fabric or lightweight flexible plastic cut into pieces 1 by 2 inches long

1. Make a copy of the butterfly kite pattern at the right, color it, and cut it out.

2. Fold along the centerline (**A**), folding the butterfly wings away from you.

3. Fold along the solid lines to the right and left of the centerline (**B** and **C**), folding the butterfly wings toward you. Crease the three folds. The newly folded, uncolored area should be on the top of the butterfly.

4. Holding the folded area on top, tape the two uncolored sides of the butterfly together.

5. Place the 5-inch piece of drinking straw perpendicular to the fold on the uncolored back of the butterfly. Tape it securely in place.

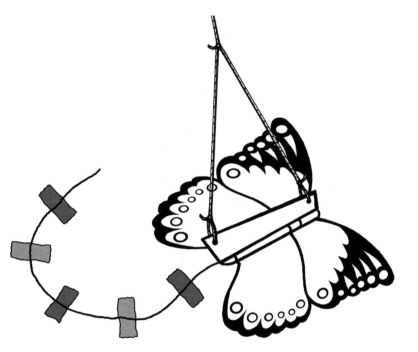

6. Punch a tiny hole at each end of the folded area on top of the butterfly. (See diagram.) Thread one end of a piece of string through one of the holes and tie it securely in place. Thread the second end of the string into the second hole and tie it securely in place.

7. Tape the second string to the backside of the kite at the center of the bottom. Tape the small pieces of fabric or plastic to the string at even intervals to make a kite tail. Adjust the position of the tail so the kite will balance when it is hung from the top string.

Display your kite where it will occasionally catch the wind and float.

DISCOVER PATTERNS MADE WITH SHAPES

Frank's design for the Coonley children's playhouse windows is shown below. Windows made from patterns of colored and clear glass are called stained glass windows. They are made from many pieces of glass held together with strips of lead. The strips of lead are shown as heavy black lines in the drawing.

It is easy to cut shapes for the colored places in the window from paper and move them around to create your own stained glass design.

The Coonley playhouse windows are made from red, blue, green, black, and clear glass. The shapes are carefully arranged on a grid of horizontal and vertical lines. One of the basic geometric shapes is missing from the design. Which one is it? The shapes work together to make a familiar object that is somewhat hidden in the window. What is it?

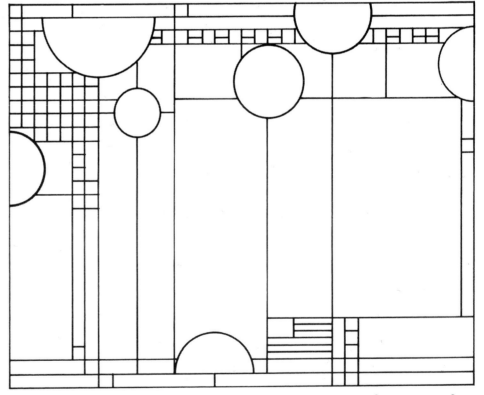

triangle, American flag

Materials

- Ruler and triangle
- Pencils
- Large sheet of white construction paper
- Several sheets of colored origami or construction paper
- Scissors
- Glue stick
- Black marker

Because you are making a design for a stained glass window, you should arrange your final design on a grid of horizontal and vertical lines. Use the ruler to draw the lines in pencil on the white construction paper. Space them 1 inch apart in each direction. Remember to leave some areas white to represent clear glass. Then cut out various geometric shapes from the colored paper. Arrange them on your grid. When you have found a design that pleases you, glue the shapes in place. Draw in the lines with a black marker connecting the shapes. The black lines represent the lead used to hold the glass in place.

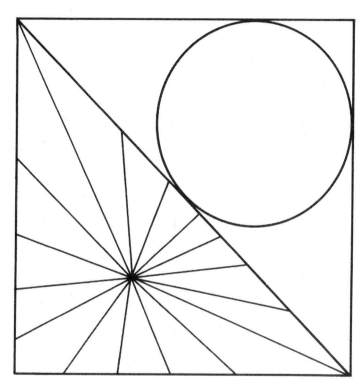

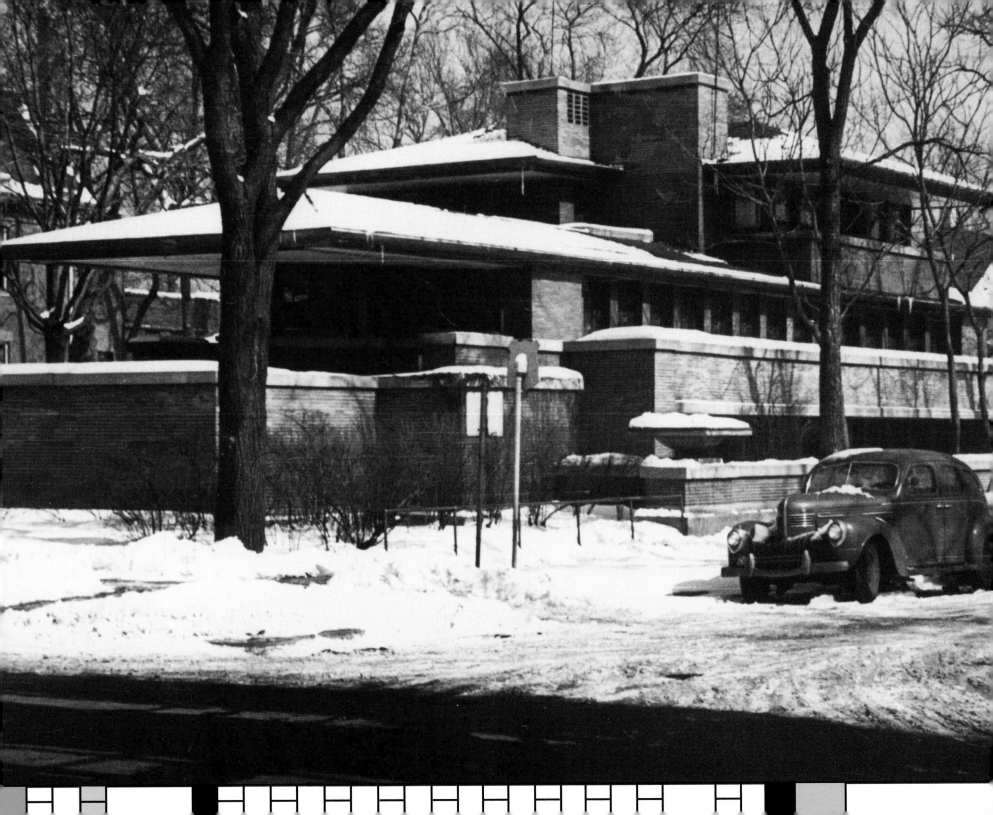

7 THE ROBIE HOUSE

IN 1908 AN INVENTOR named Frederick C. Robie drove his new motorcar around Chicago looking for an architect who would share a vision of his new house. He wanted a spacious, fire-safe house that would have fine views of the city from one large, sunny living area. His children would need a separate playroom with a safe, protected play yard. And he would need several garages for his new motorcars.

Many of the architects he visited shook their heads and told Mr. Robie he wanted one of those Frank Lloyd Wright houses. Robie's wife, Lora, approved of the idea. She greatly admired a beautiful prairie house Frank had designed in her hometown, Springfield, Illinois.

The first time Mr. Robie met Frank, he knew he had found the right architect. Frank was excited by Robie's idea of a perfect house, and Frank owned a motorcar that was nicknamed the Yellow Devil. Frank knew he had found the right client. Mr. Robie was willing to spend any amount of money to build one of Frank's prairie houses. And it was an incredible coincidence that both Frank and Mr. Robie shared an interest in motorcars. Motorcars had recently been invented, and most people were too cautious to try driving one. The two men immediately became friends of a common spirit.

Mr. Robie already owned a corner building lot in a neighborhood on the South Side of Chicago. Mr. and Mrs. Robie liked the lot, but its size and long, narrow shape presented Frank with some interesting new problems. This piece of land was much smaller than the lots

Frederick C. Robie House in winter. © *Donald Hoffman*

Frederick C. Robie drove around Chicago looking for the right architect.
The Frank Lloyd Wright Preservation Trust

The Frederick C. Robie House.
© *Paul Rocheleau*

he was used to working with, and it was tightly surrounded by the city. The house he designed for the Robies would have no open land around it. To give Mr. Robie the space he wanted, the house would have to take up the entire lot. It would be a long, narrow rectangle that was the same basic shape of his motorcar, the small vehicle that allowed him to travel with speed, comfort, and protection around the city, and also the same basic shape as a huge steamship that allows people to travel with speed, comfort, and protection across the sea.

This was a pleasing idea for Frank: a prairie house shaped like a sleek ship floating in a crowded sea of people. The shape of the house would protect it from the closeness of the city, just as the shape of a steamship protects it from the rough waters. This rectangular shape was organic. As a boy he had discovered rectangular shapes that looked like ships in the layered rocks along the Wisconsin riverbanks. Thousands of years ago, a glacier had scraped a wide path through Wisconsin and left behind beautiful layered rock formations. Many of the formations were shaped like ships made out of stone.

Frank recognized another boat shape on a common prairie plant. Every fall the flowers of the wild milkweed dried up and split open to let the wind scatter the featherlike seeds. One half of the remaining empty seed pod had the shape of a tiny boat.

Frank decided to surround the building lot with low walls to protect it from the city. Inside the walls, the long, narrow house would come to a point at either end like the prow of a ship. Steep stairs would lead from the garden to the second floor of the house. Climbing the stairs would feel like climbing up the steep side of a ship. When the top was reached, it would be like looking down on the world from a ship's deck.

To satisfy Mr. Robie, the house would be built with fireproof bricks and cement. The extra-long bricks would show the colors of the prairie clay used to make them. The vertical spaces between the bricks would be completely filled in with mortar that matched the color of the bricks. The horizontal mortar would be cut very deep to imitate the layered rock formations found in nature.

A ribbon of stained glass windows with patterns of flowers in soft prairie colors would circle the house. He would draw the wildflowers and grasses showing the hidden shapes within the outer shapes. The leaves would reach out to each other from window to window, forming a rhythmic pattern like music in the glass.

Frank could not stretch out the walls of this house to meet the prairie, but he could bring the prairie up to the walls of the house. Built-in planter boxes would be filled with seasonal flowers. Since objects found in nature are always in harmony with each other, the natural materials used to construct the walls of the house would be in perfect harmony with the flowers in the planter boxes. The flowers would grow up and overflow the walls in the same manner that wild plants grow out of small cracks in rock formations.

Frank would have a surprise for those who visited the house. It would not have a front door or any other door that could be seen from the street. At first, the visitors would wonder how to get into this odd house. They would think it outrageous. Every other proper house faced the street with its best side and had a fancy front door in the middle. The visitors might then imagine that a gangplank should be dropped down the side of the house to lead them inside.

(left) Fire-safe Robie House bricks. Horizontal spaces are deep; vertical spaces are filled in with mortar.
© Donald Hoffman

(below) The windows at either end of the Robie House form the triangular shape of the prow of a boat.
© Donald Hoffman

Fredrick Robie Jr. riding his custom-made motorcar.

The Frank Lloyd Wright Preservation Trust

Once inside, visitors would be in for more surprises. They would be drawn from the dark entrance hall to a stairway by bright light shining down from above, and they would feel like they were climbing from the dark cabin of a ship up to the bright deck. At the top of the stairs would be one big living space separated only by a huge fireplace in the same way the huge smokestack separates the main deck of a steamship. The opposite ends of the space would be pointed like the prow of a ship.

During the day the space would be flooded with light from the windows, and there would be special lights for the nighttime too. A multitude of round white sunlights spaced evenly along the sides of the room would give off light as bright as sunlight. Soft moonlights would be hidden under patterned screens on either side of the sunlights. When the moonlights were on, the room would be filled with a soft, dim glow like moonlight reflecting off water.

The windows in one wall of the playroom would come to a point to make the children feel like they were on a small play ship. They would be able to look out through the windows to a protected play yard. There would be a small garage for a custom-made toy motorcar next to Mr. Robie's giant three-car garage, which would be the largest in the world.

Construction of the Robie House began in 1908, and it was finished in 1910. It would be the masterpiece of Frank's prairie houses. Although Frank was satisfied with the Robie House, he was growing restless and discouraged with his work.

They would walk around the two sides of the house that faced the street. On the short side they would find a walkway leading to a dark cavelike space. They would think, *This could not possibly be the front door*, and walk around to the other side of the house. Here they would find large gates opening to the driveway. If the visitors chose to enter the gates, Frank would lead them through a twisting maze before allowing them to find the front door. Or, they might give up and return again to the walkway to discover that the front door was hidden, after all, in the farthest corner of the house.

READ ARCHITECTURAL PLANS TO SOLVE A MAZE

When Frank Lloyd Wright presented his clients with ideas for a new house, he needed more than words to describe his ideas. He used drawings to help them see what the house would look like.

To understand how Frank Lloyd Wright made drawings to show his clients, look at the first drawing on page 57 taken from the instruction book that came with Frank Lloyd Wright's set of Froebel blocks.

The other drawings—top view and front and side elevations—are nicknamed "the plans" and serve as the main drawings all architects must prepare when they design a house. "The plans" are shown to clients to help them understand what a house will look like, and they are shown to building contractors so they will know exactly how to build the house.

The top view is like a map of the house that tells us where everything is. Look at the floor plan for the Robie House on page 56. Architects use two parallel lines to show where the walls are. If the space between the lines is colored in, the walls extend vertically from the floor to the ceiling. If the space between the lines is open, the walls are **freestanding walls**, such as garden walls.

It is hard for first-time visitors to the Robie House to find the front door. Perhaps the house was designed this way because Mr. Robie required extra privacy; perhaps Frank Lloyd Wright wanted visitors to have the impression that they were visiting a ship. Picture a large ship in your mind. Is there a front door in the picture?

Since the Robie House is built on a corner lot, it has two sides facing the street. An ordinary house would have the front door in the center of the longest street side. Most ordinary front doors would have a porch or some kind of decoration around them making it very obvious to everyone that this is the correct place to enter the house.

The tiny footprints on the first-floor plan of the Robie House show the path a visitor has to take to find the front door if he or she chooses to enter the house from the longest street side. The only opening to the sidewalk on this side of the house is through the driveway. Pretend you are visiting the Robie House for the first time and decide to enter through the driveway. Once inside the garden walls, your long trip around the house will take you past the following items.

How many steps? How many doors (not counting the front door)? How many windows? How many trees and shrubs?

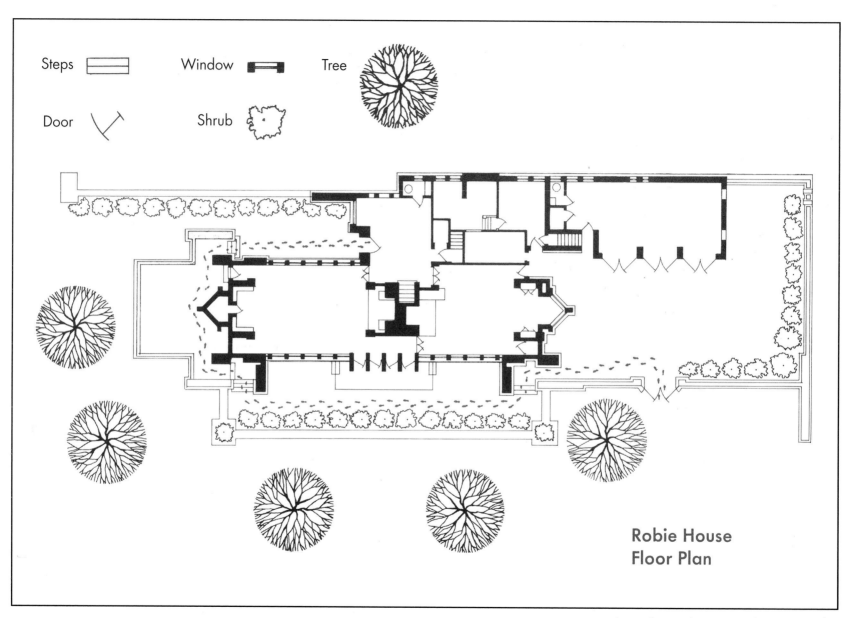

**Robie House
Floor Plan**

Steps

Window

Tree

Door

Shrub

➤ In this drawing of a little house, it is easy to see the basic geometric shapes hidden in the outer shape of the house.

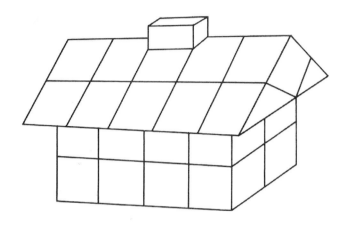

➤ If the roof and ceiling were taken off the little house and we were flying in a helicopter looking down on it, the house would look like this. It is called a "floor plan."

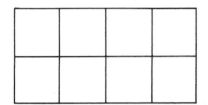

➤ If we were standing on the front side of the little house and looking straight at it, we would see this. It is called a "front elevation."

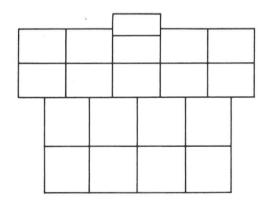

➤ If we were standing on the long side of the little house and looking straight at it, we would see this. It is called a "side elevation."

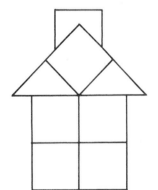

LEAVING OAK PARK

PERHAPS FRANK SHOULD have been content. Few other American architects could match his first-time accomplishments in architecture and engineering. He had shown the world his great talent for creative thinking with his designs for the Larkin Building in Buffalo, New York, and Unity Temple in Oak Park, Illinois.

Trial and Inspiration

More than ever, Frank wanted American buildings to blend organically into the American landscape, but he was losing hope that other American architects would follow his organic architecture. Perhaps Daniel Burnham had been right—it was now 1909, and most Americans turned away from his ideas. They still preferred to live, work, shop, and worship in old-fashioned buildings that copied European architecture. To make matters worse, Frank's work was often criticized. His relationship with Mamah Cheney—first a friendship but by now romantic—was scandalous and was another difficulty.

The prairie house that had once seemed like a brand-new idea to him was now very ordinary. He had "added tired to tired" and added it again and again. Frank needed time to rest and find new inspiration for his work. A European publisher offered him an opportunity. He could travel to Germany and work on a large printed portfolio of his work. Frank took the challenge. He left Oak Park to live in Europe.

Taliesin, Spring Green, Wisconsin.
Wisconsin Historical Society, Image ID 35055

Frank's departure was very difficult for Catherine and the six Wright children. Catherine's sadness grew deeper when she learned that he had taken Mamah Cheney with him. Mamah had left her husband and two very small children to live in Europe with Frank. Frank and Mamah's leaving their families created a scandal of huge proportions in Oak Park, Chicago, and beyond.

Mamah's husband took custody of their children and divorced her. Catherine hoped Frank would return to his family, and she would not agree to a divorce.

When Frank and Mamah finally returned to Chicago they were soundly criticized in every newspaper. As a result, Frank received no new work. When his mother stepped in and offered to

Frank Lloyd Wright.

The Frank Lloyd Wright Preservation Trust

Mamah Cheney

Martha "Mamah" Borthwick Cheney and her husband were neighbors and clients of Frank Lloyd Wright. Mamah shared Frank's appreciation of literature, music, poetry, philosophy, and art. At first they were friends. Then she became his mistress.

Mamah was born in 1869—just 2 years and 11 days after Frank Lloyd Wright. She was an educated woman. Educated women were less common in the early days of the 20th century, when a woman's place was considered to be in the home. Mamah earned a bachelor's degree at the University of Michigan and then worked as a librarian. She married electrical engineer Edwin Cheney in 1899. They had two children.

In 1909, Mamah left her family and lived with Frank in Europe, where she was able to be more than an Oak Park housewife. This was during the last years of the women's suffrage (right to vote) movement—a time when women's fashions and everything about women's lifestyles were rapidly changing.

While living with Frank, Mamah worked on translating the works of Ellen Key, a Swedish feminist writer. Her hopes for achievements of her own ended when she was murdered in 1914.

Mamah Borthwick Cheney, c. 1912.
Doug Steiner, The Steiner Agency Inc.

give him her share of the Lloyd Jones family land, Frank and Mamah moved to Wisconsin.

Taliesin: A New Home

The rolling hills of the Wisconsin prairie inspired Frank to build a new house. He chose a building site on the edge of a hill overlooking the beautiful valley on the Lloyd Jones family land. Frank was proud of his Welsh heritage and named his house after Taliesin, a **druid priest** who guarded the ancient religion of the British Isles. Nature was the foundation of the druids' religion, and the priests were storytellers who told the history of their people in the songs they sang.

Frank remembered his Welsh ancestors when he designed Taliesin. He built his house on the side of a hill just as an ancient fortress was built into a hill with a view over the surrounding countryside. He thought of the four basic elements of nature—earth, air, water, and fire—as he worked on the plans. The stone walls appeared to grow naturally out of the earth. The great open spaces within the walls allowed air to circulate freely. There were water fountains and a stream running through the gardens. He built huge, stone fireplaces to look like the **hearths** of his Welsh ancestors. He also planned frozen water sculptures for his house. Frost grew on the many windows and the roof pushed out beyond the walls, making perfect places for huge icicles to form in the winter.

Frank used the stones, wood, and other materials he found on his land to build Taliesin. When it was finished, the house followed the curve of

Advertisement for Midway Gardens, Chicago.
The Frank Lloyd Wright Preservation Trust

the hill and was surrounded by gardens, orchards, barns, and fields where farm crops were grown.

After a while, Frank's great talent was remembered and slowly work came back to him. He commuted to Chicago to work on new projects. One project was Midway Gardens—an elegant amusement park with extravagant outdoor gardens.

In August 1914, Frank was in Chicago working on Midway Gardens. Mamah's two children were visiting her at Taliesin. It was later reported in a newspaper article that Mamah criticized a new servant strongly and he took offense. In any case, the servant suffered a bout of temporary insanity. Catching everyone at Taliesin by surprise, he was able to murder Mamah, her two children, and four others. Two men survived the servant's attack but were badly injured. Parts of Taliesin were burned to the ground. The terrible crime devastated Frank and the local community of Spring Green. It was a long time before Frank was able to work again. Frank's son John would later say that his father never fully recovered from the horror and sadness of that day.

EXPERIMENT WITH COLORS

Frank Lloyd Wright used the rainbow of colors he found in nature to make his houses feel pleasant and comfortable for the people who lived in them. In the 1950s, he chose a group of his favorite colors and had them printed so that other people could use them in their houses. He called the colors the Taliesin Palette. Most of these colors were named after nature. The Taliesin Palette had Spring Green, Sun Tan, Raspberry, Shell Pink, Midnight, Cloud White, Bluebird, Oak Bark, Sky Blue, Autumn Green, and Cornfield Tan. These colors reminded Frank Lloyd Wright of the soft and beautiful way colors blend together in nature.

The Japanese make beautiful colored designs on paper by folding and tying paper and then dyeing it. Paper dyeing shows how the primary colors—red, yellow, and blue—blend together to form orange, green, and violet. The softness of the colors blending together on the paper reminds us of the way colors blend together in nature.

Materials

- Several medium-sized bowls
- Clean worktable protected with newspapers or a plastic cover
- Measuring spoons and cups
- Red, blue, and yellow food coloring (available at supermarkets or cake decoration stores)
- White vinegar
- Water
- 1⅛ by 24-inch pad Sumi-E Painting-Sketch paper (available at art supply stores on a continuous roll or in pads)
- Marbles
- Paper
- Rubber band

Place the mixing bowls on the table. Add 2 tablespoons of liquid or 1 teaspoon of powdered food coloring to each bowl. Add 1 tablespoon of white vinegar and ¼ cup water to each bowl. Stir to mix the colors.

Remove one sheet from the pad of paper. Handle the paper gently to avoid tearing it. Fold it into an accordion shape. Fold the accordion shape in half and quickly dip the center part in the red dye and then remove it. Unfold the paper and dip one end in the blue dye and one end in the yellow dye. Be careful not to hold the paper in the dye too long, as it will soak up too much liquid and tear.

The red and blue dyes mix together to make violet, and the red and yellow mix together to make orange. If you dye the middle of the second paper accordion yellow, what colors will you get on the ends?

Fold a second sheet of paper in half twice, use it to cover a marble, and fasten it with a rubber band. Dip the entire thing in the red dye and then dip just the tip of the marble in the blue dye.

Fold a third piece of paper in half over and over until it is a small packet. Dip each corner of the small square in a different colored dye. Set the paper aside to dry slightly for about 15 minutes so that it will not tear when you try to unfold it.

Working over the table, remove the rubber band. Slowly and carefully unfold each piece of paper and spread it out to dry. You will see that each one has a different pattern made by the dyes.

Continue to experiment with folding and color blending. The drawings below show some other tying and folding ideas. When you are finished, save your color-blending experiments. They will make beautiful wrapping paper.

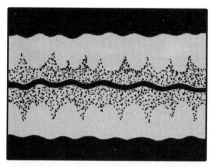
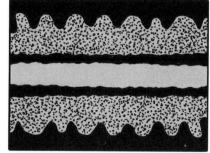
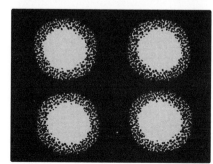
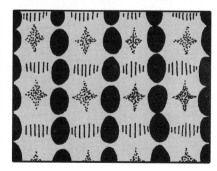

COMPARE THE DESIGN OF HOUSES

When architectural historians study houses, they look at all the things that are the same in houses that were built at about the same time. When they find a group of houses with a fairly long list of similarities, they choose a name, such as "Victorian" or "Shingle," for the houses in the group. These names are called architectural styles. Many houses have bits and pieces of different architectural styles, so these names give us only an idea of the main style of a house.

The style name of the Victorian house pictured at right is Queen Anne. This name was chosen because many houses that looked like this were built during the reign of England's Queen Anne. Frank Lloyd Wright's house is a Shingle-style house. This name was chosen because the houses in this group are usually completely covered with wooden shingles.

Have you ever wanted to know more about the houses in your neighborhood? Pictures and names of some of the main styles of American houses are shown on the following pages. Try matching the houses on your block to these architectural styles.

Queen Anne Victorian

Colonial

English

Craftsman Bunglalow

Spanish

Prairie

Beaux Arts

Modern

© Julius Shulman

Storybook

A NEW BEGINNING

WHEN PUBLIC OPINION WAS against him and Frank had very little work, several projects came his way that offered him some new challenges and fresh inspiration. A wealthy heiress named Aline Barnsdall picked him as the best architect to design several buildings for her. She had recently purchased a large piece of land, known as Olive Hill, near the center of Los Angeles. She planned to build a theater, a children's playhouse, apartments for actors and artists, and a small shopping center on Olive Hill. The first step in the ambitious project was a large new home for her family.

Traveling through the western United States on his way to Los Angeles, Frank saw a different American landscape. Rock formations and mountains rose up from the sweeping flat desert land to meet the endless blue sky. The red, violet, and orange colors of the sunrise and sunset were brilliant against the soft gold, brown, and green colors of the desert.

Olive Hill, true to its name, was covered with soft gray-green olive trees. From the top of the hill, it was possible to see great distances through the clear, dry desert air. Frank placed the house so it would have views of the ocean, the mountains, and the tall buildings of downtown Los Angeles. He designed it to look as naturally a part of Olive Hill as rock formations are a part of mountainsides. Because of the warm Los Angeles weather, the gardens surrounding the house stayed green all year long and were pleasant places to spend time, even in the winter.

Aline Barnsdall
and her daughter.

*City of Los Angeles Cultural
Affairs Department.
Gift of David and
Michael Devine*

Aline Barnsdall was an agreeable client, but there were problems from the very beginning. She spent all of her time traveling around the world. At this time in Frank's life, he was always traveling too. In 1914 he had been chosen to design an important project in Tokyo, Japan—the Imperial Hotel. Work on the impressive hotel continued for many years. During these years, Frank traveled frequently to Tokyo. Frank and Aline discussed plans for the new house in letters and telegrams they sent each other all over the world.

Later Frank wrote in his autobiography, "I would hear from [Aline] when I was wandering around in the maze of the Imperial Hotel in Tokyo and she was in Hollywood. She would get my telegram in Spain when I eventually got to Hollywood. And I would hear from her in New York while I was in Chicago or San Francisco. Or, she would write to me from a camp in the Rocky Mountains when I was seasick out on the Pacific Ocean."

Aline made an unusual request in one of her letters. She wanted to use her favorite flower, the hollyhock, in the decorations Frank planned for her house.

When the house was finished, visitors saw real hollyhocks growing in the gardens, and they saw Frank's architectural hollyhocks. He had simplified the flowers, leaves, and stem to the basic geometric shapes of the Froebel blocks, and then he had decorated the house with geometric flowers. Cast concrete hollyhocks grew from the corners of the roof. A pattern of hollyhocks was pressed into the plaster that covered the outside walls. Inside the house, concrete hollyhocks grew on the living room walls, and hollyhocks were carved into the backs of the dining room chairs. Hollyhocks were woven into the carpets that covered the floors. Some visitors thought they could even see hollyhocks hidden in the stained glass windows. In fact, there were so many hollyhocks in Aline's house that it was soon nicknamed the Hollyhock House.

Frank designed a mysterious entrance to the Hollyhock House. A dark, low walkway led to a small cavelike hall that opened into a large, bright living space. The high ceiling was shaped and painted to feel like a soft desert landscape. Glass doors and windows brought light and a view of the surrounding gardens inside the house. The four natural elements—earth, air, fire, and water—were found at the giant fireplace. Earth was the concrete stones used to build it. Light and air filtered down from a skylight above. Fire burned within the hearth. A tiny horseshoe-shaped pond of running water separated the fireplace from the rest of the room. Frank decorated the space above the hearth with a design that showed shapes he found in nature simplified to the basic geometric shapes of the Froebel blocks: the circle, the square, and the triangle.

Frank, who created wonderful playrooms for the children who lived in his houses, made a special place for Aline's daughter, Sugar Top. Because Sugar Top was a very little girl living in a very big house, he made part of the house feel like it was just her size. Sugar Top had her own child-sized bedroom, bathroom, dressing room, and play porch. Frank did more than make the rooms the right size for a child. He created a place in the dressing room that Sugar Top could imagine was her very own private tree house. From the sunny, open play porch windows, she looked out to her very own child-sized garden.

Aline and Sugar Top lived in their beautiful new house for only a short time. Soon Aline discovered that she could not be happy living in just one place. Frank was disappointed when she asked him to stop working on her project. He had already drawn plans for a theater building, and construction work on a children's playhouse and two smaller houses for Olive Hill was under way. A few years later, Aline gave Hollyhock House and most of Olive Hill as a gift to the City of Los Angeles. She wanted it to be saved as a place for children to learn about art and the theater. To this day, the Hollyhock House is open to the children and people of Los Angeles as a museum, a gallery, and an art school.

Working with Concrete

Frank stayed in Los Angeles and continued to build concrete houses. Concrete was a good building material to use in the desert. It was cheap, it looked like stone, and it was easy to shape. Frank showed his skills as both engineer and architect when he invented a way of holding hollow concrete blocks together with strong steel rods. Steel woven through concrete made a building material that reminded Frank of spiderwebs. Four houses built in Los Angeles from Frank's blocks are nicknamed

A pattern of concrete hollyhocks decorates the Hollyhock House.
© Donald Hoffman

Living room with giant fireplace and pond, Hollyhock House.
© Larry Underhill

69

the Textile Block houses. This is another way of saying that the houses are woven together to make them strong in the same way threads are woven together to make a fabric strong.

The hollow concrete building blocks reminded Frank of another object found in nature. A seashell is decorated with beautiful patterns, and it provides a home for the creature that lives inside.

In the same way that nature provides beautiful housing for small sea creatures, Frank decorated the outside of his concrete block shells and used them for both the inside and outside walls of the Textile Block houses. These houses were a new accomplishment for Frank and he was pleased with them, but, in general, the rest of his work and his personal life did not go as well.

Sugar Top on the steps of the Hollyhock House.
City of Los Angeles Cultural Affairs Department. Gift of David and Michael Devine

Inside courtyard, Hollyhock House.
© *Julius Shulman*

DRAW REALISTIC AND ABSTRACT FLOWERS

The flowers Frank Lloyd Wright used to decorate the Hollyhock House were simplified to the basic shapes of the Froebel blocks. Some of the flowers that decorate the house are drawn using plane geometry, and some use shapes from solid geometry.

There is not much difference between the photograph of a hollyhock shown here on the left and the first drawing on page 72, because both the photograph and drawing are **realistic** pictures that show us how hollyhocks look when they have length, width, and thickness. We see the flowers as shapes in solid geometry.

In the second drawing, the flower shapes have only length and width. They are shapes in plane geometry. In the last drawing, the flower has been drawn using only flat geometric shapes. The process of simplifying shapes from the very realistic, shaded shapes of solid geometry to the flat, one-color shapes of plane geometry is called abstraction.

Frank Lloyd Wright simplified or abstracted the realistic shapes of a real hollyhock flower to the flat geometric shapes of the flowers he used to decorate the Hollyhock House. We do not know how many drawings he made before he drew the final patterns for the **abstract** hollyhocks, but if we work with a photograph and several drawings, we can begin to see the process he used.

On a clean sheet of paper, draw a tulip flower using the basic geometric shapes in the same way Frank Lloyd Wright drew the hollyhock flower.

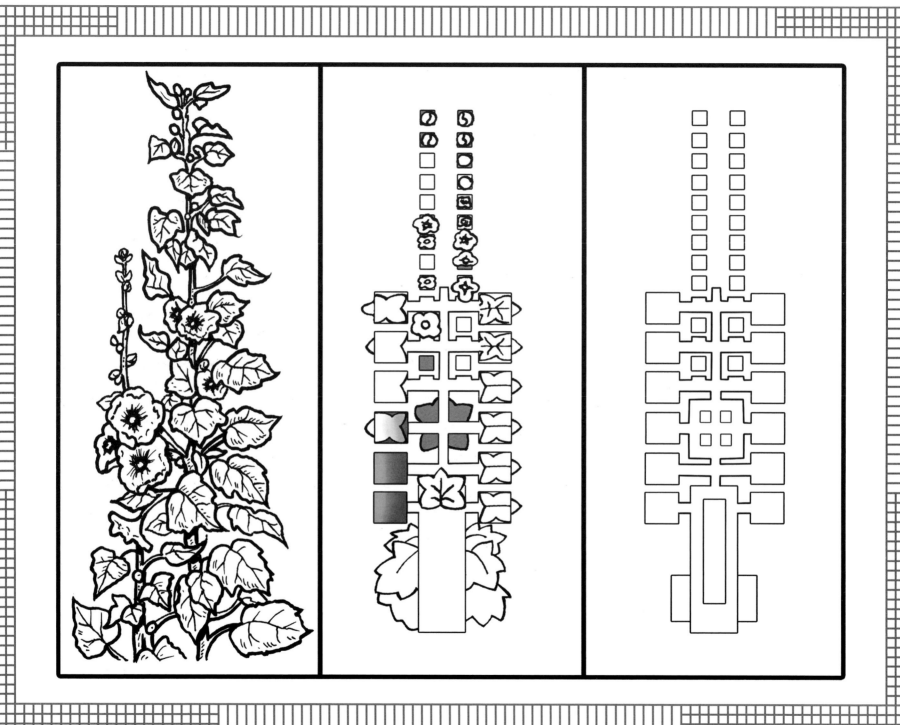

MAKE A MODEL TEXTILE BLOCK FROM PLASTER

The geometric hollyhocks on the outside walls of the Hollyhock House were made or cast in a mold. A mold is a space that has the negative shape of the sculpture. The textile blocks also were cast in a mold. Both hollyhocks and textile blocks are relief sculptures, which are carved by hand or cast in a mold. We cannot see all sides of a relief sculpture because it is attached to a flat background.

The idea of positive and negative shapes is easier to understand in plane geometry. Drawing 1 shows a positive shape in white against a dark background. Drawing 2 shows the same shape as a negative, dark shape against a white background.

In solid geometry, the positive shape represents the sculpture. The negative shape represents the space into which the sculpture would fit exactly, or its mold.

1

2

You can experiment with making relief sculptures in your kitchen.

Materials

▶ Worktable covered with newspaper or plastic

▶ Aluminum foil baking pan, 8 by 3¾ by 2½ inches, one for each sculpture

▶ Bag of sand, 5 pounds (gather at the beach or purchase at a pet or hardware store)

▶ Ruler

▶ Water

▶ Spatula

▶ Tools for shaping sand (buttons, empty spools of thread, thimbles, forks, spoons, bottoms of glasses or other dishes and small pans, dice, balls, pencils, rulers, Lego blocks, Lincoln logs, screwdrivers, nails, and pliers)

▶ Bag of plaster, 5 pounds (purchase at a hardware store)

▶ Old bowl

▶ Large old spoon

▶ Scissors

▶ Old toothbrush or small paintbrush

➤ Cover your worktable with newspaper or heavy plastic to protect it from your work materials. Fill the aluminum foil baking pan with 1 inch of sand.

Wet the sand with enough water to make it firm, not soupy. If the sand is too dry, you will not be able to shape it. If it is too wet, your shape will sink back into the sand. Mix the sand thoroughly and smooth the top with a spatula until it is level.

Use your tools to make a design in the sand. Press the tools firmly into the sand, but do not dig through to the bottom of the sand. If you dig through to the bottom, the plaster will run through and spoil your sculpture.

Smooth the surface of the sand and try other designs. Look at the pictures of the hollyhocks and textile blocks. Just for fun, try to re-create one in the sand. When you have made a design that you like, it is time to mix the plaster.

74

Plaster is mixed in the proportion of 2 cups of water to 3 cups of plaster. To make a small batch, put 2 cups of water in the bowl and add 3 cups of plaster. Do not put the plaster in the bowl before the water because the plaster will not mix properly. Quickly stir the mixture until there are no lumps.

Carefully dribble the plaster into the deepest places in your design. When they are filled, dribble—do not pour—the plaster over the sand until it is completely covered. If the plaster begins to harden, throw it away and mix a new batch. Do not try to thin the plaster by adding more water.

When the sand is completely covered with dribbled plaster, you may gently pour the plaster into the mold. Pour plaster in the mold until the ½-inch space at the top is filled. Level the top with the spatula. If the first batch of plaster did not fill your mold completely, mix a second batch and pour it into the mold as long as the sand is completely covered with the first batch.

It will take about an hour for your mold to dry. During that hour, the plaster will harden and feel cold to the touch; then it will feel warm. When the plaster feels cold a second time, you can turn your sculpture out of the mold. Cut down the corners of the pan and peel away the sides. Carefully turn out the mold onto a piece of newspaper.

Let the mold dry for another half hour and gently brush off the excess sand with the toothbrush. As you brush, your design will begin to appear. Gather up the excess sand and save it to use again.

It will take your sculpture several days to dry completely. As it dries, the sculpture will become lighter in weight, and the sand will become lighter in color. Until the plaster is completely dried out, a few grains of sand will come off when you touch your sculpture. When it is completely dry, no more sand will rub off.

10 MODERN ARCHITECTURE

THE 1920s WERE TRYING times. With great hope for new accomplishments, Frank began work on many interesting projects: a huge ranch, a resort in Lake Tahoe, a hotel and elaborate water gardens in Arizona, a 32-story skyscraper in Chicago, a planetarium in Baltimore, and a fantastic 150-story cathedral and skyscraper. Every one of these projects was canceled. Sometimes Frank was not even paid for his work, making life very difficult for him.

After more than a decade of living apart, Catherine divorced Frank in 1922. The divorce allowed Frank, now aged 56, to marry an artist named Miriam Noel. Unfortunately, Miriam and Frank were unhappy and soon separated.

One night Frank attended the Chicago opera and was seated next to a charming young dancer named Olgivanna Lazovich Hinzenberg, a fascinating and bright woman. Frank was taken with her. Legally he was still married to Miriam, who was jealous of Frank's relationship with the younger Olgivanna. Miriam tormented Frank and even had him put in jail. It was the second time that Frank's personal life made scandalous newspaper headlines.

In 1925 a daughter was born to Olgivanna and Frank. They named her Iovanna. The family now numbered four including Svetlana, Olgivanna's daughter from a previous marriage. Three years later, after Frank was divorced from Miriam Noel, he and Olgivanna were married in California.

Frank spent one happy winter working on a hotel called San Marcos in the Desert. Frank and his drafting assistants set up a temporary camp in the desert near

The Bogk House at dusk.
© *Paul Rocheleau*

Olgivanna Lazovich Hinzenberg.
Wisconsin Historical Society,
Image ID 87748

Frank Lloyd Wright, age 63.
Wisconsin Historical Society,
Image ID 1921

the hotel. They built tents from cheap lumber and canvas fabric and painted them red to match the desert sunset. When the camp was finished, they named it "Ocatillo" after a cactus that blooms with bright red flowers. From a distance, Ocatillo looked like a group of giant red butterflies resting on the black desert rocks.

When the stock market crash struck the United States in 1929 and a serious economic depression followed, almost all Americans had hard times. The only client for new architectural work was the U.S. government, and the government jobs always went to traditional architects. Experimental architects like Frank had absolutely no work. During the Great Depression, not everything was bad for Frank, however. He was invited to exhibit his work in a show at the Museum of Modern Art in New York. Frank was to be a smaller part of the exhibit, which featured European Bauhaus architects—the Swiss Le Corbusier, and the Germans Mies van der Rohe and Walter Gropius. Although Frank was not one of the major architects, it was important that he was invited to participate.

New Students and New Ideas

Frank spent the depression years writing his autobiography and giving speeches on his favorite subject, organic architecture. Olgivanna encouraged him to open an architectural school where Frank could train young architects to design organic buildings when America began to build again.

The couple's home Taliesin, which had been rebuilt after it was destroyed by fire, was enlarged to make room for students and classroom/studios. The first year the school, which Frank called the Taliesin Fellowship, was open, 23 students came from all over the world. Frank planned unusual classes for them. They learned by making things with their hands. Students were expected to become skilled at many different crafts: woodworking, glassmaking, pottery, textiles, landscaping, sculpture, painting, drama, music, and dance.

Learning to work together was another important part of student life, because a successful architect must be able to work with others. Students were responsible for running the Taliesin farm and for building new additions to the house, school, and barns. Students did housework, cooked and served meals, cared for the flower gardens, and grew their own food in the vegetable garden. While the students "added tired to tired," they liked to sing a song written by Frank called the "T-Square and Triangle Work Song."

As the years passed, Frank grew more and more concerned about the problems of overcrowded American cities. He believed that city life would be more peaceful if every family had wide open space surrounding them. With the help of his students, he created an imaginary city that he hoped would show his fellow Americans how city life could be improved with good architectural design. There would be no crime, no racism, no political demonstrations, no pollution, no crowding, and no money problems in Frank's imaginary city. Every family would have a small piece of land to farm. There would be small apartments for single people, small shopping centers, small businesses, little factories, and little schools because he believed that citizens who are surrounded by open space and nature will live a happier life.

Frank called this imaginary place Broadacre City. A model of it toured the United States during the 1930s. The model was a great social success because Americans who saw it began thinking of ways to improve their cities. It was a personal success for Frank because it brought him respect from his fellow Americans.

View of Wisconsin countryside, Taliesin East.
© *Paul Rocheleau*

Taliesin students loading hay.
© *Pedro Guerrero*

Design Ideas from Germany

The Bauhaus School (1919–1933) was an art school founded in Germany by modernist architect Walter Gropius (1883–1969). Mies van der Rohe, a member of the faculty, would later say, "The Bauhaus was not an institution with a clear program—it was an idea, and [Walter] Gropius formulated this idea with great precision. . . . The fact that it was an idea, I think, is the cause of this enormous influence the Bauhaus had on every progressive school around the globe. . . . Only an idea spreads so far."

The Bauhaus curriculum combined crafts and the fine arts and later architecture, furniture design, graphic design, interior design, industrial design, photography, and typography. After the school closed in Germany, it was re-established in Chicago as the New Bauhaus or the Institute of Design, which is still famous for taking a revolutionary approach to education. In general, Bauhaus designs were simplified forms with no decorations applied to surfaces.

Walter Gropius moved to the United States, but instead of settling in Chicago with Mies van der Rohe and other Bauhaus teachers, he took a teaching position at the Harvard Graduate School of Design. He is remembered as early master of modern architecture.

Charles-Édouard Jeanneret (1887–1965), known professionally as Le Corbusier, was a European modernist architect who was associated with the Bauhaus. He is remembered for his excellent work as an architect, an urbanist, a furniture designer, and a writer.

Ludwig Mies van der Rohe (1886–1969) was a German-born modernist architect and furniture designer. He was the last director of the Bauhaus in Germany. When the school closed because of events that led to World War II, he moved to Chicago to become director of the architecture school at the Illinois Institute of Technology. Mies is remembered for his Barcelona Pavilion in Barcelona, Spain; Seagram's Building in New York City; Crown Hall in Chicago; and the quote, "Less is more."

S. R. Crown Hall, 1959, campus of the Illinois Institute of Technology, Chicago, Illinois, Ludwig Mies van der Rohe, architect.
Illinois Institute of Technology

DESIGN A CITY

Frank and his students developed a plan for an imaginary place where families could live happier lives on small farms where they would be close to nature. Try your hand at designing a city of your own.

Materials

▸ Clear tape

▸ Several sheets of blue line graph paper, 5 squares to the inch

▸ Clean desk or flat work surface

▸ Drafting tape

▸ Small pad of tracing paper (optional)

▸ Several sharp 2H drawing pencils

▸ Eraser

▸ Ruler

▸ Small architectural template (This is very inexpensive and may be purchased at an art or stationery store.)

▸ Assorted colored pencils

Have you ever played with an electric train? When you laid down the track did you plan a place for a tunnel, a bridge, and a station? Did you also think about the farms, factories, and houses your train would pass on its journey around your room? When you stood up and looked at your train layout from above, you were looking at it in the same way an architect or city planner looks at a plan view. This is also the same way we look at a map.

In a plan view, all of the buildings, trees, and roads are shown with different geometric symbols. Using simple geometric shapes, you can plan an imaginary city on paper in the same way. First, you need to decide what buildings you want in your city. It should have houses and apartment buildings for people to live in. It should also have public buildings—places where people can get together to learn, work, play, shop, and worship. On the following page is a list of buildings and symbols that are usually found in a small American city. Since this is probably the first time you have tried to design a city, it is a good idea to choose only a few items from the list.

Your city must also have transportation or a way for the people who live there to travel around. Bicycles, motorcycles, cars, trucks, buses, and trains are some of the ways people who live in cities travel from place to place. When you plan your city, you will need to make a path for transportation.

Geometric shapes are an easy way to show where the different places in your city can be found on a plan view. For example, houses can be shown with small squares and a roadway or train tracks with parallel lines. The symbols will give you some ideas of how to show buildings in a plan view.

Before you begin planning your city, you will need to tape four sheets of graph paper together to make one big sheet. Tape the big sheet of graph paper to the table with drafting tape. After you lay out all of your supplies on the table, you are ready to begin.

Imagine that you are in an airplane flying over a large piece of open land. It may be flat or hilly. It may be dry desert land or green prairie. Where will you put the roads and buildings? Where are the trees and parks? Where will people live?

Before architects draw finished designs on paper, they sketch out their ideas on tracing paper. If you have a pad of tracing paper, tape a sheet of it over the graph paper and use it to sketch out your plan. You may erase or choose to use a new sheet of tracing paper over the first one as you plan your city. When the design is finished, draw the design carefully on the graph paper using a ruler and the template. Now you may color your drawing.

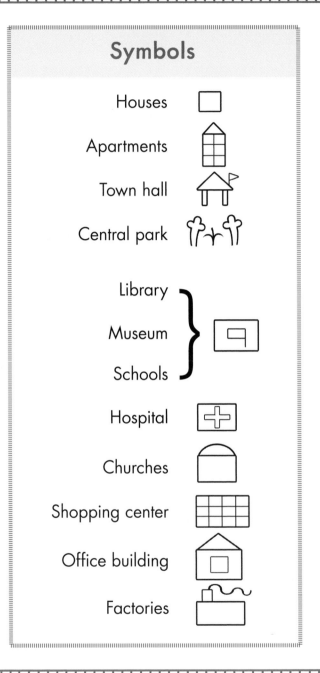

Symbols

Houses

Apartments

Town hall

Central park

Library
Museum
Schools

Hospital

Churches

Shopping center

Office building

Factories

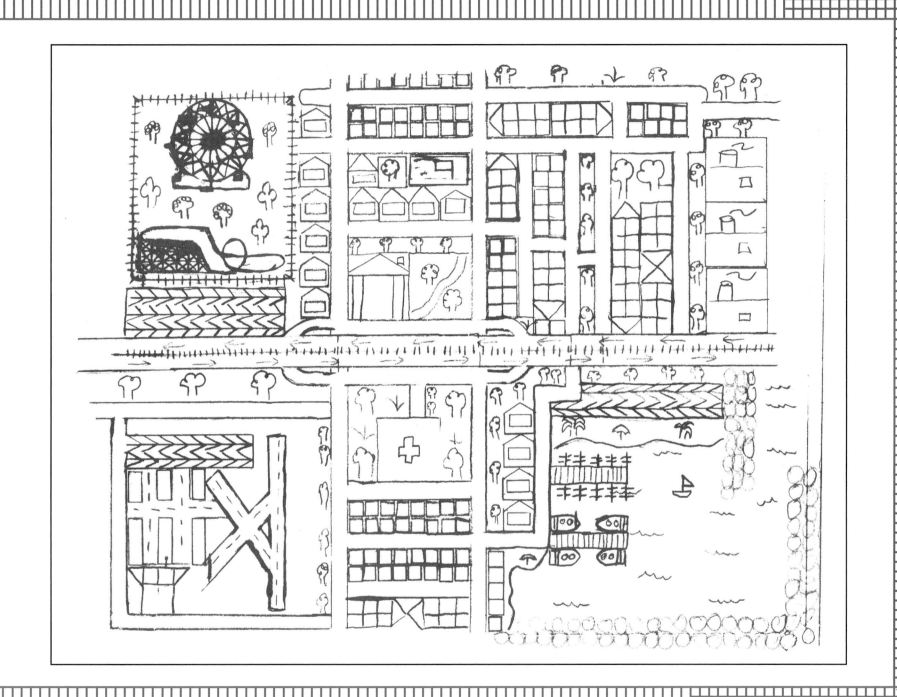

Fallingwater

Money to pay for the traveling exhibit of Broad-acre City was contributed by the parents of Edgar Kaufmann Jr., one of Frank's students. In 1934, the Kaufmanns invited Frank to visit their weekend cabin in Mill Run, Pennsylvania. Frank's imagination was captured by the beautiful sight of water falling over a rocky ledge in a stream named Bear Run. The waterfall was a favorite gathering place for the Kaufmann family because they enjoyed the great beauty of nature they found there.

When Frank returned home to Taliesin he often thought about Bear Run and the music he heard in the sound of its falling water. A house began to take shape in his mind, a house that would be part of nature's music. If the Kaufmanns agreed, he would design a house that would be

View of Fallingwater
from downstream.
© *Paul Rocheleau*

built on the giant rocky ledge above the water-fall. The rocky ledge would "root" the house to the earth in the same way roots firmly attach a tree to the earth. The house would cantilever or extend out over the waterfall in the same way a tree branch extends out from the trunk of a tree. In fact, the house Frank dreamed of would be like a tree house, which is part of nature but also a safe place for people to live. Frank planned to build the house using materials he found on the Kaufmanns' land. These natural materials would blend in perfect organic harmony with the music of the stream and the other parts of nature.

The Kaufmann House would appear to float in the air above the waterfall. The fireplace would rise out of the giant rock that would root the house to the earth. The four basic elements—earth, air, fire, and water—would come together in the Kaufmann House to show the great contrasts Frank saw in nature: light and dark, earth and air, and fire and water. The Kaufmann House would show that it is possible for men and women to live in complete harmony with nature.

Frank wrote a long letter to the Kaufmann family describing the house he wanted to build over the waterfall on Bear Run. The Kaufmanns were excited by his ideas and wrote back asking him to prepare sketches of the house. This was the last time Frank worked on the house until Mr.

Kaufmann telephoned him one morning at Taliesin from nearby Milwaukee. "I am on my way to see you," he said, "and I am looking forward to looking at the sketches of the house you described in your letter." Frank immediately sat down and began drawing. When Mr. Kaufmann arrived, Frank took him to the dining room for lunch. While they ate and took a tour of the Taliesin farm, Frank's students drew up the first plans for the house. Later in the afternoon, Frank proudly showed Mr. Kaufmann sketches and drawings for his new house. The amazing end to this story is that the Kaufmann House, called Fallingwater, was built almost exactly as Frank drew it that morning.

Living room of Fallingwater. The hearth is built on the rocky ledge of the waterfall.

© Donald Hoffman

85

BUILD A CANTILEVER AND A MODEL OF FALLINGWATER WITH GRAHAM CRACKERS

Fallingwater is probably Frank Lloyd Wright's most famous house. Fallingwater's closeness to nature and its position right over a waterfall make the house unforgettable, but when we look at a picture of Fallingwater, the thing we notice first are the **cantilevers**. *The cantilevers make the house look like a tree growing over a waterfall. Tree branches are cantilevers made by nature. The branch is attached or supported at one end only—at the trunk. A diving board is another example of a cantilever—an object that extends out into space and is supported at only one end.*

You can build a cantilever with objects you find around your house. Bricks or blocks will work very well. You will need six to eight rectangular blocks of the same size. Make a base of three blocks and place a fourth block on top of them at a right angle. This block will fall off unless you support it at one end with one or two more blocks. When block number four is held in place without the help of your hand, you have made a cantilever.

Graham crackers are a perfect size and shape for building cantilevers. You can build a model of Fallingwater using graham crackers and a cement called Royal Icing.

Graham Cracker Fallingwater

Materials

- Waxed paper
- Royal Icing (see recipe below)
- Box of graham crackers
- Spatula
- Cardboard for base

Tear off a large piece of waxed paper and lay it down on a clean table. You will build your model on the waxed paper. If any icing drips down from your model, it will stick to the waxed paper instead of the table. When the model is finished, it will be easy to remove the waxed paper from the bottom. You will risk breaking the model if it dries stuck to the table.

Practice building a cantilever with the graham crackers, so you will know how many crackers are needed to hold up a cantilever of one cracker.

Now, looking at the picture of Fallingwater, build your model. When the model is finished, allow it to sit untouched for two hours in a dry place. This will give the Royal Icing a chance to dry. After you are finished admiring your model, you can eat it.

Royal Icing Recipe

Ingredients

- 3½ cups confectioners' sugar
- 2 egg whites
- ½ teaspoon cream of tartar
- 2 tablespoons lemon juice (optional)

Utensils

- Electric mixer with bowl
- Measuring spoons
- Rubber spatula
- Spoon or knife
- Container with tight-fitting lid

Combine the sugar, egg whites, and cream of tartar in a mixing bowl and beat with an electric mixer set on low speed until the ingredients are blended together. If you like, you can add lemon juice for additional flavor. Then beat at high speed for 7 to 10 minutes. The icing is ready to use when you can draw a spoon or knife through it and the icing holds its shape.

Royal Icing becomes very hard when it dries. Store it in a container with a tight-fitting cover.

LISTEN FOR SOUNDS MADE BY WATER

Frank Lloyd Wright thought of his organic houses as a meeting place for the four elements: earth, air, fire, and water. Perhaps water is the most interesting because it takes many different shapes. For example, water is the only element we can find as a solid, a liquid, and a gas in the earth's atmosphere at the same time. If this seems impossible to you, imagine yourself on a humid day, standing next to a swimming pool holding a glass filled with ice cubes. The humidity, pool water, and ice are all different forms of water. Humidity is water as a gas; the pool contains water as a liquid; and the ice is water as a solid.

When Frank Lloyd Wright first visited the waterfall on Bear Run, he heard the music made by nature in the sound of falling water. If you close your eyes and think of the sound a waterfall makes, it is easy to understand why. Have you ever really thought about the sounds—or music—water makes in nature?

There are two lists in the box. The first one is a list of water words. The second is a list of words that describe sounds made by water. Fold a piece of lined paper in half to divide the lined spaces into two columns. Write the water words in the left-hand column, skipping a line between each word. Now write a word in the right-hand column that makes you think of the sound made by the water word. Continue down the list of water words, matching a sound to each word. Since some water words have many sounds, you may want to use some of the words more than once. Remember that music has rests or silent places. When you are listening for music in nature, think of silence as a part of nature's music.

Water Words	Water Sounds
waterfall	bubbling
icicle	pounding
ice	silent
snow	hissing
frost	cracking
fog	tinkling
rain	splashing
surf	crunching
stream	raging
hail	pattering
waves	lapping
cloud	dripping
geyser	pouring
river	rushing
brook	babbling
run	sprinkling

As Frank grew older, it became harder for him to live through the cold Wisconsin winters. He loved the warm, dry Arizona desert and decided his school could divide the year equally between Taliesin in Wisconsin and a warmer Taliesin West in Arizona. In 1937, Frank bought a piece of land 26 miles from Phoenix on a great flat **tabletop mesa** in the mountains. Standing on his new land was for him like being on top of the world.

Because the desert had bold shapes and was very bare, Frank designed his house and new school buildings with sharp angles and hard lines to match the surrounding desert. His students built Taliesin West with their own hands. When they were finished, the buildings looked as though they had stood in the desert for hundreds of years, as natural as the rocks on mountain slopes. Remembering his Ocatillo camp, Frank used canvas for the tops and sides of the buildings so that the rooms would be open to let the desert air flow through.

Usonian Houses: Building for Everyone

By the late 1930s the United States slowly recovered from the Great Depression. Frank had new architectural projects. One of them was surprising.

He had designed many houses for rich clients. Now he thought about houses that could be built for Americans of average wealth income. This idea took shape in Frank's Usonian style. The first Usonian house was built in 1936 in Madison, Wisconsin, for Herbert and Katherine Jacobs.

Lloyd Wright playing the piano inside one of the Ocatillo tents.
Wisconsin Historical Society, Image ID 86852

Since the Jacobs family had very little money to spend on a new house, Frank saved money by making the house very simple. There was no basement. Hot water pipes buried underneath the floor to heat the house acted like a giant hot water bottle in the winter. This method of heating is called radiant heat. The walls were ready-made sandwiches of building materials that workers could quickly put in place, and the roof was **insulation** squeezed between layers of roofing material. Electrical wires, plumbing, and gas pipes were all located in the same place. The family car was parked in an open carport. All of these money-saving construction tricks helped Frank build the Jacobs family a very fine house for a small amount of money.

(above) Jacobs House, Madison, Wisconsin.
© Paul Rocheleau

(right) Living room of the Jacobs House.
© Paul Rocheleau

Even though the Jacobs House cost very little to build, it was in every way as beautiful as Frank's other houses. Like the Winslow House, one of the first houses Frank designed after leaving Louis Sullivan's office, the roof of the Jacobs Usonian House appeared to float over the house. Frank made this happen with a band of windows placed along the top of the walls just under the roof. There was a large fireplace in the center of the open living space, and large glass windows looked out on a private garden. The basic elements of nature were in the simple Jacobs Usonian House just as they had been in the houses Wright designed for his wealthier clients.

Just like the Winslow House, the Jacobs Usonian House became a popular sightseeing attraction. So many people knocked on the Jacobs' door and asked to see the house that the family began charging an admission fee. Frank designed more Usonian houses that were built all over America. In fact, Frank's Usonian houses were the very first American ranch-style houses.

In the same year, 1936, Frank designed a second Usonian house for Paul and Jean Hanna, professors at Stanford University in Palo Alto, California. Nature was still a source of inspiration for Frank. For this house he borrowed a theme from a tiny creature that fascinates children—the honeybee. The house was based on the six-sided **hexagon** that makes up the tiny cells of the honeycomb. Everything in the Hannas' Honeycomb House—even the tables and beds—was a hexagon or a part of a hexagon. In keeping with the inspiration for their house, the Hanna family kept honeybee hives in the gardens.

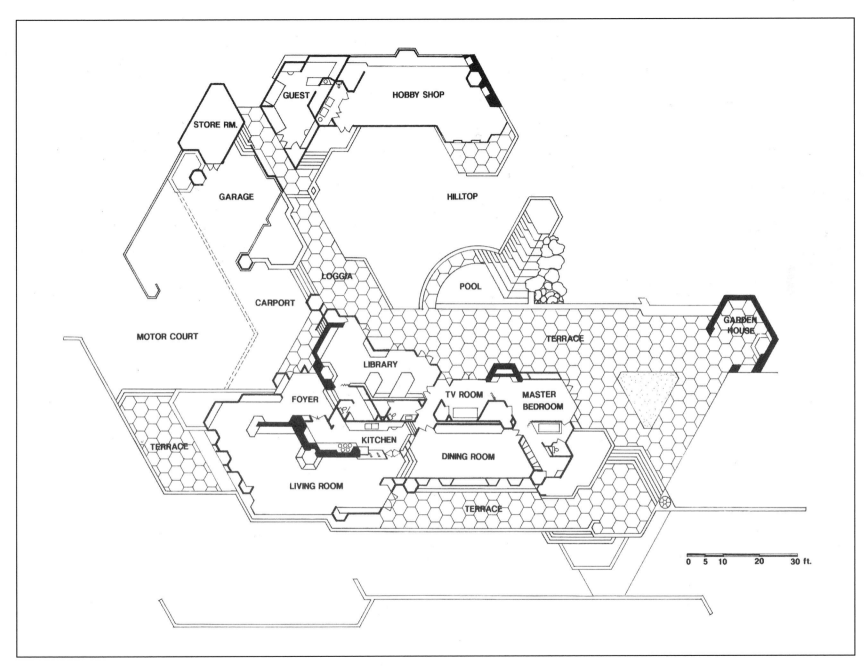

Floor plan, Hannah "Honeycomb" House, Palo Alto, California.

Office of James Graham Pulliam, F.A.I.A.

DESIGN WITH HEXAGONS

Almost all houses are made from square shapes. Because Frank Lloyd Wright liked to try out new ideas, he experimented with making houses from non-square shapes. Perhaps his most interesting non-square houses were the hexagonal houses.

He saw the shape of regular six-sided hexagons inside bee hives. Bees make their honey storage places in this shape because the hexagon is nature's best way of making a storage space. Frank Lloyd Wright thought nature's best way of making a storage space would also be the best way of using space for family living.

Since all the angles in a hexagon are greater than the angles in a triangle or square, there is more room to store things in the corners. This is why bees make their hives from hexagon shapes. Perhaps the reason that only a few of these unusual hexagonal houses were built is it is very difficult to match the many sides of many hexagons together perfectly. Anyone who has stitched a grandmother's flower garden quilt—a pattern made from tiny hexagons—knows how hard it is to match enough of these six-sided shapes together to cover a bed.

Oyster or soup crackers are usually made in the shape of small regular hexagons, and they can help you experiment with making shapes from hexagons.

Materials

- Hexagon-shaped oyster or soup crackers (such as Nabisco's New England oyster crackers)
- White cardboard
- Fast or quick-drying white glue
- Paints and a paintbrush

Spill some of the crackers onto the board and play with them until you have made a design that pleases you.

Dab a small amount of glue on the back of each cracker and press it firmly in place on the cardboard. Let the glue dry. Now you may paint your design if you wish.

Now try building your own hexagon shapes.

Materials

- Pipe cleaners, any color
- Drinking straws, or cocktail straws if you can find them (clear or a solid color will look best)
- Worktable
- Old scissors
- Quick-drying white glue
- Tissue paper, any color you like

Spill the pipe cleaners and drinking straws onto the table.

Cut the pipe cleaners and straws exactly in half. Bend the pipe cleaners in half and use them to join the drinking straws together into the shapes of hexagons. When you have made a design that pleases you and one that has symmetry—when one side of a line drawn down the center is exactly the same as the other side—run a small line of glue all along the straws and a dab at each joint. Place a sheet of tissue paper over your design and press down to join the glue with the straws. Allow time to dry. Cut around the outer edge of your shape.

Make your design into a kite by adding a string and a tail.

II HOUSES FOR YOUNG PEOPLE

FRANK HAD ALWAYS REMEMBERED to include a place for children in the houses he designed for families. It is not surprising that he accepted two very young people as clients.

A Persistent Young Fan

Seth Peterson was born in a small town in western Wisconsin. As a boy he was interested in architecture, especially the work of the famous architect who spent his summers in a neighboring town. When he was old enough, Seth applied to the Taliesin Fellowship for admission as a student-apprentice. Unfortunately, the school did not have a place for him. Seth didn't give up. He continued to stay in touch with Frank, asking him several times to design a Seth Peterson house. Frank declined. He was 90 years old and far too busy with other work. Finally, Seth sent Frank a check as a down payment on a house design. Frank, who always needed money, spent Seth's check and so finally agreed to draw plans for a very small cottage on a lake.

Seth owned a piece of wooded land near Mirror Lake in Wisconsin. Frank's plans placed the house on the edge of a hill above a lake. Frank designed a cottage with a combined living room and kitchen, a bedroom, and a bathroom. He chose native Wisconsin sandstone for the walls of the house. The sandstone matched the bluffs that surrounded it. He rooted the house to the earth with a giant chimney. He decorated a row of

Seth Peterson Cottage, Mirror Lake State Park, Wisconsin.
© Kit Hogan

95

Seth Peterson Cottage interior.
© *Kit Hogan*

and researched its history. When it was discovered that Frank Lloyd Wright was the architect, funds were raised and the cottage was restored. Today it is as beautiful as Frank and Seth Peterson planned it to be and the cottage is available for rent.

The Wright Doghouse

The Berger family lived in a rented house in northern California during the late 1940s. They rented a house because they were waiting for Mr. Berger to finish building a Usonian house that Frank had designed for them. Jim, the older of the Bergers' two boys, loved his dog—a large black lab named Edward or "Eddie." The lab wasn't allowed in the house, but he was allowed to sleep in the basement.

In 1950 the new house was ready and the Berger family moved in. The house was lovely, but there was no inside place for a dog to sleep. Frank didn't believe in basements because he thought they were places to store items that should really be thrown away. Edward didn't fit into that category, however. He had to sleep in the workshop area of the new house.

For several years, Jim worried about Edward sleeping in the workshop. Finally, he asked his dad to build a doghouse. But what would the doghouse look like? It had to match the Bergers' new house. Jim's mother suggested, "Why don't you write to Mr. Wright? After all he is the architect who designed our house. Perhaps he has an idea for a dog-sized house."

ribbon windows with a pattern of abstract cutout pine trees. In other words, Frank was still using nature as the inspiration for his work.

Sadly, both Frank and Seth Peterson died before the cottage was completed. Seth was only 24. Over the years the cottage fell slowly into disrepair. The land it stood on was purchased by the State of Wisconsin and added to Mirror Lake State Park. No one seemed to remember Seth's cottage was there. In the late 1980s a canoeist paddling in Mirror Lake discovered a curious dilapidated structure. The canoeist took an interest in the old building

So Jim did just that. Here is the letter he sent Frank in 1957:

> June 19, 1956
>
> Dear Mr. Wright:
>
> I am a boy of twelve years. My name is Jim Berger. You designed a house for my father whose name is Bob Berger. I have a paper route which I make a little bit of money for the bank, and expenses.
>
> I would appreciate it if you would design me a dog house, which would be easy to build, but would go with our house. My dog's name is Edward, but we call him Eddie. He is four years old or in dog life 28 years. He is a Labrador retriever. He is two and a half feet high and three feet long. The reason I would like this dog house is for the winters mainly. My dad said if you design the dog house he will help me build it. But if you design the dog house, I will pay you for the plans and materials out of the money I get from my route.
>
> Respectfully yours,
> Jim Berger

Frank was an old man at the time, and he was very busy with many projects including the Guggenheim Museum in New York. But he found time to answer Jim Berger. Here is the letter Frank sent to Jim.

> June 28, 1956
>
> Jim Berger
> Box 437
> San Anselmo, California
>
> Dear Jim:
>
> A house for Eddie is an opportunity. Some day I shall design one but just now I am too busy to concentrate on it. You write me next November to Phoenix, Arizona and I may have something then.
>
> Truly yours,
> Frank Lloyd Wright

Jim wrote Frank on the first of November, and Frank returned his letter with a drawing of a triangular doghouse to match the Bergers' triangle-themed house. By the time Frank's plans for a doghouse arrived, Eddie had found a favorite place to sleep. The Bergers' Usonian house was heated with radiant heat—hot water running through pipes under the floor. Eddie discovered that the floor of the front porch was also warmed by radiant heat. The porch was covered so he was protected from the rain. It was quite a pleasant spot. He didn't need a doghouse.

The Bergers' next dog was an Irish setter named Shaughnessy. Mr. Berger finally built the triangular doghouse and Shaughnessy used it—sometimes. By this time Jim Berger had grown up and moved away from home. He never forgot his experience with Frank Lloyd Wright.

A triangular doghouse designed by Frank Lloyd Wright.
Courtesy of Jim Berger

SEARCH FOR CLUES TO THE HISTORY OF OLD HOUSES

Most historic houses that have been designed by famous architects like Frank Lloyd Wright and are open for the public to tour have been "restored." This means that the buildings have been returned to the way they looked in the past. This is not always the way they looked the year they were built. It can be, as in the case of President Harry Truman's house in Independence, Missouri, the way the house was when President Truman and his wife Bess last lived in it in the late 1950s, even though the Victorian house was originally built in the late 1800s.

People who restore houses must first decide on the year they wish to return the house to. In the case of private houses, the decision is made by the owners. In the case of house museums, the decision is made by the people who run the museum.

Most old houses have changed in one way or another over time. They may have belonged to several different families who had different needs and tastes in home decoration. Many of them have been remodeled. Rooms have been added or removed to make way for different sized families. Kitchens and bathrooms have changed to make room for new appliances and different family lifestyles.

When a house is restored as a museum, careful studies are made of the way the house used to look. Restoration research is usually done by a specialist or professional architect, but it can also be done by you. If you live in an old house or know someone who does, you can be a detective and search for clues to the past history of the house.

Materials

▶ Notepad

▶ Pencils

▶ Strong flashlight

Be sure you have the permission and assistance of an adult who lives in the house before you begin your search. Don't remove anything from the walls without adult permission and assistance. If a suitable old house is not easy for you to find, ask your parents to take you to a local historical house that is open for tours. A docent will usually explain the discovery of clues and the story of the restoration during the tour.

Begin by talking to the owner of the house. Write down your information on the notepad. Ask if the owner has the building plans. Check at the local building department (usually found in the city hall) to see if permits for additions to the house were issued. Old photographs and conversations with people who used to live in the house can provide valuable clues to what the house looked like long ago.

Old toilets are usually marked with the date they were made.

Windows can help identify the date a house was built and show where changes have been made to a house. It is common for colonial-style houses to have windows made from many separate panes of glass that are all the same size. Each individual pane of glass is called a "light," and the windows are called six-light or eight-light windows. The date a colonial house was built can be determined by the number of window lights.

Different window styles help identify places where a house has been changed. It is easy to spot household remodeling that was done after 1945 because it was popular to use louver windows and sliding glass doors at that time.

Pieces of old wallpaper or paint colors may be hidden under light switch plates and mounted wall fixtures. Sometimes they can be found in closets, under mirrors, or behind built-in drawers and inside window seats. These clues will tell you the original color of the walls.

Search the basement or attic with a flashlight. Basements usually have more clues than attics. Look for old pipes or wires that were left behind when the house was remodeled. They can show you where a kitchen sink was located or where walls have been moved. Look for the foundation of a chimney that may have been removed from the top floors of the house. Look for notes with dates that have been written on the walls by workmen.

When you have finished your search, write a brief history of the house and the changes that have been made to it. Be sure to include the date the house was built and the date of your search.

12 FINAL YEARS

IN THE 1930s A VERY LARGE project came to Frank from the S. C. Johnson & Son Company in Racine, Wisconsin. Frank had been without a substantial piece of work for years, and the Johnson's Wax project brought him great joy. He later recalled:

When the sky at Taliesin was dark and the days there gloomy . . . came a note from Hib [Herbert Johnson] enclosing a retainer (one thousand dollars) [$16,400 now]. . . . And, the pie thus opened, the birds began to sing again below the house at Taliesin; dry grass on the hillside turned green, and the hollyhocks went gaily into a second blooming. The orchard decided to come in with a heavy crop of big red apples and the whole landscape seemed to have more color. . . . Ideas came tumbling up and out onto paper. . . . But at once I knew the scheme I wanted to try.

The building Frank designed for Johnson's Wax (today named S. C. Johnson) borrowed some ideas from the Larkin Building. Both buildings were located in unattractive industrial areas. For this reason Frank used nature in the inside of the buildings. He wanted the people who used the buildings to see the beauty of nature that was missing from their outside surroundings.

Frank was still playing tricks on the eye. The entrance to the Johnson's Wax building was through an area with a low ceiling that opened onto a spacious,

Illustration of Fir Tree House showing the hat or tree above the roofline.
Painting by Greg Allegretti, A.I.A.

brightly lighted, multistory space. Visitors had the sensation that they were outside with the sky above and a forest growing all around. A skylight at the top provided the sky effect, and gigantic tree-shaped supports provided the illusion of trees. It was then and still is today an amazing sight to see.

In 1945 Frank was asked to design a vacation home on the Pecos River in northern New Mexico. The house offered him a new opportunity to design a house in a wild natural setting—a setting as beautiful as Fallingwater. The Pecos River flows through the heavily forested Santa Fe National Forest. One side of the river is grassy land; the other side is a steep wall of stone. Frank's design for the vacation house reflected the local geography.

Frank chose native stone and wood shingles as building material. The house had two enormous chimneys. Massive chimneys still represented the center of family life to Frank. One side of the house wore a tall triangular top hat that had the shape of the nearby mountains. It also had the shape of a tree. Today the house is known as the Fir Tree House. For more than 50 years few people noticed the house that was so very different from neighboring summer cabins. Then one day an architect on his way to fish for trout in the Pecos River recognized the gate to the house as the work of Frank Lloyd Wright. Word spread.

The Guggenheim

Solomon R. Guggenheim was a wealthy New Yorker. He had a fine collection of modern art and wanted to build a museum where he could display his collection. Guggenheim wanted a building that would be a temple of the spirit, a monument. Frank gave him one. In fact, when construction of the museum was completed, the public would sometimes take more notice of the building than of Guggenheim's art collection.

Frank was 76 years old when he began work on the Guggenheim. He had not changed the basic beliefs of his youth and his respect for nature. It is not surprising that Frank chose a spiral-shaped shell—a chambered nautilus or common garden snail—as the outer shape of the new museum. But what would Guggenheim have thought if his famous architect presented him with the idea of a building shaped like a huge garden snail? Instead, Frank presented the idea for a building that would be shaped like a ziggurat. Ziggurats were towering structures built near temples in ancient Mesopotamia (present-day Iraq). They resembled the shape of a wedding cake, because each new layer was smaller than the last. Frank's design would turn the wedding cake shape upside-down, however, resembling a snail. He quipped that it was hard to look a snail in the face since he had stolen the idea of its house—from its back.

Plans for building the new museum met with a lot of criticism. It was difficult to find exactly the right building lot in New York City, which was already crowded with buildings. The New York building code did not allow for a structure like this to be built. The fact that it would stand had to be proven by Frank's engineers. It took many years to clear the way for the actual construction of the museum.

Frank incorporated two of his favorite geometric shapes—the circle and the triangle—throughout the museum. In the circular-shaped skylight, triangular shapes are discovered. Lights are recessed or hidden in the ceiling and covered by triangular pieces of glass. The lobby floor has a pattern of circles. The staircase is built in the shape of a triangle.

The Guggenheim finally opened on October 21, 1959. When visitors arrived they walked into

(above) The spiral shape of a chambered nautilus shell.

(below) Guggenheim skylight.
© *Kathleen Thorne-Thomsen*

a soaring lobby space. Light shone down on them from a great height above. They looked up to see a giant skylight composed of 12 pie-shaped sections—like the rays of the sun. After visitors finished admiring the lobby space, a nearby elevator carried them to the top. From here they would look down and see the lobby area far below. When they were ready they would begin to walk down the spiral ramp. Along the way, Frank had created small personal areas for viewing paintings and other pieces of art. Visitors could look at the nearby art or turn around and gaze across the vast central space at other visitors who were doing the same thing on the other side. In this way Frank achieved two things: a feeling of being alone for very private appreciation of art and a feeling of being part of a community with the other visitors who were observed at all levels of the spiral ramp.

The Guggenheim received a lot of attention when it finally opened. Not all of the attention was good. Artists complained that their work would not be viewed properly. The sloping, curving walls and spiral ramp walkway made every piece of art displayed there appear to be out of perspective. Hanging paintings in this wildly curvy environment took special skills and experimentation to get it right. When a painting looked straight it was actually crooked.

(below) Guggenheim levels, inside.
© *Kathleen Thorne-Thomsen*

(right) Guggenheim cartoon from *The New Yorker* magazine. Cartoon drawn by James Stevenson.
© *The Cartoon Bank*

The Guggenheim Museum in New York City was one of Frank's last projects. He worked on the museum for 16 years. Unfortunately, he died six months before his famous museum formally opened in October 1959.

A Space-Aged Work

In 1960, neighbors who lived near a large grassy field in Wauwatosa, Wisconsin, saw an odd shape rise from the ground. They were curious and kept an eye on it. Word spread. People from all over Milwaukee wondered what was being built on the edge of their city. Families made special trips to watch the progress of the building.

At first they watched the construction of a giant concrete cross with four equal legs. Then the concrete was finished in the color of stone that is native to the area. The color made the cross look as though it had grown out of the earth. After that, workmen built a huge dome-shaped roof on top of the cross. The roof was finished in a bright blue color—just like the sky. Rays like the spokes of a wheel cantilevered from the edge of the dome. The rays were joined with a repeating pattern of cutout semicircles. Under the dome and all around the circle were semicircles of stained glass. Just before the building was finished, workmen dug a circular pond.

When it was finished, it really looked as though a giant spaceship had landed in a large grassy field next to a round pond in Wauwatosa. What was it? Everyone wondered. If the building has stained

Illustration from the April 1959 issue of *Newsweek* magazine.

glass, they thought, it must be a church. It was a church—Annunciation Greek Orthodox Church, designed by Wisconsin's most famous architect, Frank Lloyd Wright.

The congregation of Annunciation had hired Frank to design their new building four years earlier, in 1956. The project must have been of special interest to Frank because his wife, Olgivanna, had grown up in a family that practiced the Greek

The Space Race

In the late 1950s the Space Race was underway, and all Americans were very aware of outer space. The Russians launched the world's first satellite, Sputnik 1, into orbit on October 4, 1957. The Space Age began with Sputnik's success. Space Age shapes—comets, stars, orbiting planets—and images of imaginative space ships were used in all areas of design. Do you think Frank's design for Annunciation Greek Orthodox Church fit into the Space Age theme of the late 1950s?

Annunciation Greek Orthodox Church in Wauwatosa, Wisconsin.
Author's collection

Orthodox religion. Frank also remembered a masterpiece of Byzantine architecture: Hagia Sophia, an Eastern Orthodox cathedral in Istanbul, Turkey, built in 360 AD. A massive circular dome is one of the outstanding features of Hagia Sophia.

Frank decided to use a circle—one of the basic geometric shapes—as the basic element of the new church. The shape of the Greek cross would form the base of the circular dome. A circular reflecting pool in the front would mirror the image of the church, the dome, and the sky. Inside the church the dome space would be free of supports, allowing all 750 worshipers to see clearly in all directions.

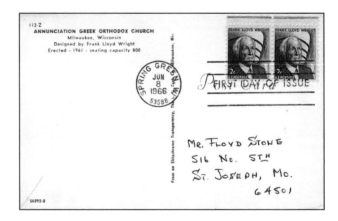

First-day-of-issue stamps celebrating Frank Lloyd Wright's birthday and the Guggenheim Museum.
Author's collection

Final Days

Happy times at the Taliesin Fellowship were spent celebrating festivals that reminded Frank of the Lloyd Jones family Sunday gatherings he loved as a child. Every summer the students returned to Taliesin in time to celebrate Frank's birthday on June 8 by setting off fireworks and floating hundreds of small candles on the Taliesin pond.

Another Fellowship favorite was the Easter festival celebrated at Taliesin West. Sometimes as many as 150 guests were invited to join the festivities. Easter Sunday began with breakfast. Tables were set up outside and decorated with flowers and brightly colored Easter eggs. All of the guests dressed in fine outfits, but the women were always the center of attention; they wore fantastic, self-decorated hats. After breakfast, the students sang and then asked the guests to join them in singing

Easter hymns. In 1959, Frank became sick at Eastertime. With his family and friends surrounding him, he died peacefully on April 9, 1959.

Frank Lloyd Wright had worked as an architect for 72 years, "adding tired to tired" and sticking to his ideas even when everyone was against him. He is sometimes called the Father of American Architecture. Sightseers travel from all over the world to see his best-known houses, the Home and Studio in Oak Park, Illinois; the Robie House in Chicago; the Hollyhock House in Los Angeles; and Fallingwater in Mill Run, Pennsylvania. Perhaps we can best remember Frank Lloyd Wright in his own words: "We must study nature," he said. "It can reveal principles, form, design, the inner rhythm of all being. . . . A genius is a man who has an eye to see nature, a man with a heart to feel nature, a man with the boldness to follow nature."

Frank Lloyd Wright's funeral in Wisconsin.

Wisconsin Historical Society, photo by Milwaukee Journal Sentinel, *Image ID 5137*

Frank Lloyd Wright was a hard worker, but when his work was finished, he loved to have a good time. He gave big parties. The students of the Taliesin Fellowship sometimes worked for days preparing decorations, costumes, and food for Frank Lloyd Wright's celebrations. Music and a poem or a reading from one of his favorite books were also parts of the celebrations.

These activities give you ideas about music, poetry, food, drink, and table decorations that will help you plan your own small seasonal festivals, one to celebrate spring and one to revel in winter. Check with your parents to arrange a time for your festival. Perhaps you could decorate the table and help prepare the dessert for a special family dinner. Maybe you could invite two or three friends over for an afternoon party. These seasonal festivals can be celebrated during the quiet times of the year when there are no birthdays or holidays. You can substitute the poems for your favorite poems or stories. If you do, try to pick some music to go along with them.

PLAN A SPRING FESTIVAL

➤ Russian composer Modest Moussorgsky's music called "Night on Bald Mountain" and "Claire de Lune" by French composer Claude Debussy will paint musical pictures that will help you imagine the following humorous poem.

➤ Serve cinnamon muffins with orange spice iced tea.

➤ A basket filled with tall green grass is a perfect decoration for a spring table.

The Wind and the Moon

Said the Wind to the Moon, "I will blow you out;
You stare in the air
Like a ghost in a chair,
Always looking what I am about—
I hate to be watched; I'll blow you out."

The Wind blew hard, and out went the Moon.
So, deep on a heap
Of clouds to sleep,
Down lay the Wind, and slumbered soon,
Muttering low, "I've done for that Moon."

He turned in his bed; she was there again!
On high in the sky,
With her one ghost eye,
The Moon shone white and alive and plain.
Said the Wind, "I will blow you out again."

The Wind blew hard, and the Moon grew dim.
"With my sledge, and my wedge,
I have knocked off her edge!
If only I blow right fierce and grim,
The creature will soon be dimmer than dim."

He blew and he blew, and she thinned to a thread.
"One puff more's enough
To blow her to snuff!
One good puff more where the last was bred,
And glimmer, glimmer, glum will go the thread."

He blew a great blast, and the thread was gone.
In the air nowhere
Was a moonbeam bare;
Far off and harmless the shy stars shone—
Sure and certain the Moon was gone!

The Wind he took to his revels once more;
On down, in town,
Like a merry-mad clown,
He leaped and halloed with whistle and roar—
"What's that?" The glimmering thread once more!

He flew in a rage—he danced and he blew;
But in vain was the pain
Of his bursting brain;
For still the broader the Moon-scrap grew,
The broader he swelled his big cheeks and blew.

Slowly she grew—till she filled the night,
And shone on her throne
In the sky alone,
A matchless, wonderful silvery light,
Radiant and lovely, the queen of the night.

Said the Wind: "What a marvel of power am I!
With my breath, good faith!
I blew her to death—
First blew her away right out of the sky—
Then blew her in; what strength have I!"

But the Moon she knew nothing about the affair;
For high in the sky,
With her one white eye,
Motionless, miles above the air,
She had never heard the great Wind blare.

—George Macdonald

Cinnamon Muffins

Ingredients

Muffins

- Butter for greasing muffin tin
- ¼ cup butter
- 1 extra-large egg
- ½ cup milk
- 1½ cups all-purpose flour
- 2¼ teaspoons baking powder
- ¼ teaspoon salt
- ⅓ cup white sugar
- ½ teaspoon nutmeg

Topping

- ⅓ cup butter
- 1 teaspoon cinnamon
- ⅓ cup white sugar

Utensils

- Muffin pan
- Small saucepan
- Mixing bowls and spoon
- Measuring cups and spoons
- Flour sifter
- Hot pads
- Cooling rack

This recipe makes 10 to 12 muffins.

Preheat the oven to 425°. Set all ingredients and utensils out on a clean working space. Grease the muffin pan generously with butter.

Melt ¼ cup butter in a saucepan over a low flame on the stove. You may also melt the butter in a bowl in a microwave.

Break the egg into a small bowl and beat it with a fork until the white and yolk are thoroughly combined. Stir the ½ cup milk into the beaten egg. Stir the melted butter into the egg and milk mixture.

Sift together the flour, baking powder, salt, sugar, and nutmeg in a medium-sized bowl. Make a small hole in the center of the flour mixture and pour the egg, milk, and butter mixture into it. With the mixing spoon, stir only enough to wet all of the flour mixture. The muffin batter should be lumpy.

Spoon equal amounts of batter into the well in the muffin pan. Place the pan in the middle of the oven and bake for 12 minutes.

Prepare the topping while the muffins are baking. Melt ⅓ cup butter in a small saucepan. Mix the cinnamon and sugar in a small bowl. Set both the saucepan and bowl on the table.

The muffins are done when the tops are golden brown. Remove the muffins from the pan and cool them on a rack for a few minutes. When the muffins are cool enough to touch, dip the top of each muffin first in the butter and then in the sugar and cinnamon mixture.

Serve the warm cinnamon muffins in a basket that has been lined with a pretty dish towel.

Orange Spice Iced Tea

Ingredients

- Water
- 2 orange spice tea bags
- Ice cubes
- Sugar cubes

Utensils

- Tea kettle
- Teapot
- Hot pads
- Pitcher
- Tall glasses

Fill the tea kettle with cold water and bring the water to a boil.

Fill the teapot with boiling water and let it warm the pot for a minute or two. Pour the water back into the tea kettle and bring the water to a boil again.

Put the tea bags in the teapot and fill it with boiling water. Cover the teapot with a tea cozy or a dish towel and let the tea steep for about 5 minutes.

Allow the tea to cool to room temperature. Pour the tea into a pitcher filled with ice cubes. Fill the tall glasses with the tea and add more ice cubes. Serve with sugar cubes.

Makes 4 servings.

A Basket of Spring Grass

You can grow thick, healthy grass in less than a week from wheat seeds. The supplies you will need are usually sold at feed stores and nurseries. If you have trouble finding either of them, you can substitute rye grass seed and potting soil.

Materials

- Large basket or bowl-shaped flowerpot
- Heavy plastic wrap
- 1 pound vermiculite or potting soil
- 1 pound wheat seed or rye grass seed
- Large pan

Line the basket with plastic wrap. Fill it with vermiculite, leaving a 2-inch space at the top to put the seed. Sprinkle the wheat seed on top of the vermiculite.

Set the basket in a sink and add water until the seed feels moist. You will not need to water it again for at least a week unless you live in a desert climate.

Set the basket on a pan in a warm place where it will get filtered sunlight. To keep the wheat seed moist, cover the basket loosely with plastic wrap. Remove the plastic wrap after 2 days. The seeds should take a few more days to grow.

PLAN A WINTER FESTIVAL

➤ Claude Debussy wrote a collection of short piano pieces for children called the "Children's Corner Suite." The fourth and fifth pieces, "The Snow Is Dancing" and "Golliwogs Cakewalk," will help you imagine the scene in the following poem of dancing potatoes on a winter evening. Another beautiful piece of music that accompanies prancing potatoes and a cold night is "Pavane" by Gabriel Faure. It is easy to imagine the druid priests singing this tale to children in the early days of the British Isles.

➤ Serve geometric shape cookies with warm milk and honey.

The Potatoes' Dance

I

"Down cellar," said the cricket,
"Down cellar," said the cricket,
"Down cellar," said the cricket,
"I saw a ball last night,
In honor of a lady,
In honor of a lady,
In honor of a lady,
Whose wings were pearly white.
The breath of bitter weather,
The breath of bitter weather,
The breath of bitter weather,

Had smashed the cellar pane.
We entertained a drift of leaves,
We entertained a drift of leaves,
We entertained a drift of leaves,
And then of snow and rain.
But we were dressed for winter,
But we were dressed for winter,
But we were dressed for winter,
And loved to hear it blow.
In honor of the lady,
In honor of the lady,
In honor of the lady,

Who makes potatoes grow,
Our guest the Irish lady,
The tiny Irish lady,
The airy Irish lady,
Who makes potatoes grow.

II

"Potatoes were the waiters,
Potatoes were the waiters,
Potatoes were the waiters,
Potatoes were the band,
Potatoes were the dancers
Kicking up the sand,
Kicking up the sand,
Kicking up the sand,
Potatoes were the dancers
Kicking up the sand.
Their legs were old burnt matches,

Their legs were old burnt matches,
Their legs were old burnt matches,
Their arms were just the same.
They jigged and whirled and scrambled,
Jigged and whirled and scrambled,
Jigged and whirled and scrambled,
In honor of the dame,
The noble Irish lady
Who makes potatoes dance,
The witty Irish lady,
The saucy Irish lady
Who makes potatoes prance."

—Vachel Lindsay

Geometric Shape Cookies

Adult supervision required

Ingredients

▶ Butter or margarine for greasing the cookie sheets
▶ 1 cup butter
▶ 1 cup sugar (white or brown)
▶ 1 extra-large egg
▶ 1 teaspoon vanilla
▶ 2 tablespoons cream
▶ 3 cups all-purpose flour
▶ 1 teaspoon baking powder
▶ $\frac{1}{8}$ teaspoon salt
▶ White Buttercream Frosting (recipe page 115)
▶ Nonpareils (for decoration)

Utensils

▶ 2 cookie sheets
▶ Plastic or metal measuring cups
▶ Electric mixer with mixing bowl
▶ Measuring spoons
▶ Rubber spatula
▶ Rolling pin and pastry cloth
▶ Knife
▶ Cooling rack
▶ Hot pads

This recipe will make four dozen small cookies. Baking time is 8 to 10 minutes, and the preheated oven temperature is 350°.

Lightly grease the cookie sheets with butter.

Put 1 cup of butter in a large mixing bowl. Beat with an electric mixer until the butter is fluffy and light in color.

Add 1 cup of sugar to the butter, and beat for 1 or 2 minutes.

Add the egg to the mixing bowl and beat just enough to mix it in.

Measure the vanilla and cream and beat them into the mixture.

Sift the flour, baking powder, and salt together and gradually add to the mixture in the bowl.

When all the flour is mixed into the dough, cover the bowl tightly with plastic wrap and refrigerate for 1 hour.

Divide the dough into four equal balls. Place the dough, one ball at a time, on lightly floured pastry cloth. Sprinkle a little flour on top of the dough and roll it out to about $\frac{1}{8}$ of an inch thick. If you lift the rolling pin slightly as you reach the edge, the dough will not crack or split on the edges.

Use the knife to cut cookies in geometric shapes and carefully transfer them to a cold, lightly greased baking sheet. Bake only one baking sheet of cookies in the oven at a time.

Bake in a 350° oven for 8 to 10 minutes until the cookies are a light brown around the edges. Using hot pads, remove the baking sheet from the oven and let the cookies cool for 5 minutes before moving them from the baking sheet to a cooling rack with a spatula.

You may roll your dough scraps a second and third time and make more cookies from them. Top the cookies with the buttercream frosting.

White Buttercream Frosting

Ingredients

- 4 tablespoons melted butter
- 1 teaspoon vanilla
- 1 tablespoon lemon juice
- 1-pound box sifted powdered sugar
- Water or milk

Utensils

- Small saucepan
- Small mixing bowls
- Measuring spoons
- Electric mixer with bowl
- Rubber spatula
- Table knife

Melt the butter in a small saucepan.

Mix the melted butter, vanilla, lemon juice, and sugar in a small mixing bowl until the frosting is smooth. If the frosting is too stiff, add a small amount of water or milk to make it thin enough to spread on the cookies.

When the cookies are no longer warm to the touch, frost them using the table knife. Put the nonpareils (either white or multicolored) in a small bowl and press the frosted cookies into them before the frosting hardens.

Warm Milk with Honey

Ingredients

- 4 cups milk
- ½ cup honey
- 1 teaspoon vanilla

Utensils

- Glass measuring cup
- Plastic or metal measuring cups
- Measuring spoons
- Medium saucepan
- Wooden spoon
- Hot pads
- 4 mugs

Measure the milk and pour it into the saucepan. Heat it over a low flame until bubbles begin to form around the sides of the pan. Add honey and vanilla and stir with the wooden spoon until they are dissolved. Pour the sweetened milk into the mugs and serve warm.

Makes 4 servings.

WORK A CROSSWORD PUZZLE

Yiou learned all of the words in this crossword puzzle while you read the story of Frank Lloyd Wright's life. If you need help remembering the words, the page number where the word appears is given as a hint. Rather than writing in this book, photocopy the puzzle and write your answers on that copy. Hint: the glossary at the end of this book will help you.

Across

2. An object in the ceiling that lets sunlight into a room. (Hint: page 42)

5. This building material is an important part of modern buildings. In 1906, Frank Lloyd Wright was the first architect to use it as the main building material for a large building. (Hint: page 42)

8. A part of a building that extends from the building in the same way a tree branch extends from the trunk of a tree. (Hint: page 85)

9. An open porch with a roof over it that is often found along the sides of a Victorian house. (Hint: page 21)

10. The last name of the creator of Frank Lloyd Wright's favorite childhood building blocks. (Hint: page 2)

11. The nickname for Frank Lloyd Wright's woven concrete blocks. (Hint: page 70)

Down

1. In the early 1900s, the main living areas of most houses were divided into many little rooms. Frank Lloyd Wright's houses were different because the main living area had one large space just like the great American _____ spaces. (Hint: page 22)

3. A private place to sit next to the fireplace. (Hint: page 22)

4. A part of a Victorian house that rises up way beyond the roof. People can usually walk up into it and see for a great distance. (Hint: Page 21)

6. Another word for fireplace. (Hint: page 61)

7. The word Frank Lloyd Wright used to describe the way he designed his houses to be in perfect harmony with nature. (Hint: page 21)

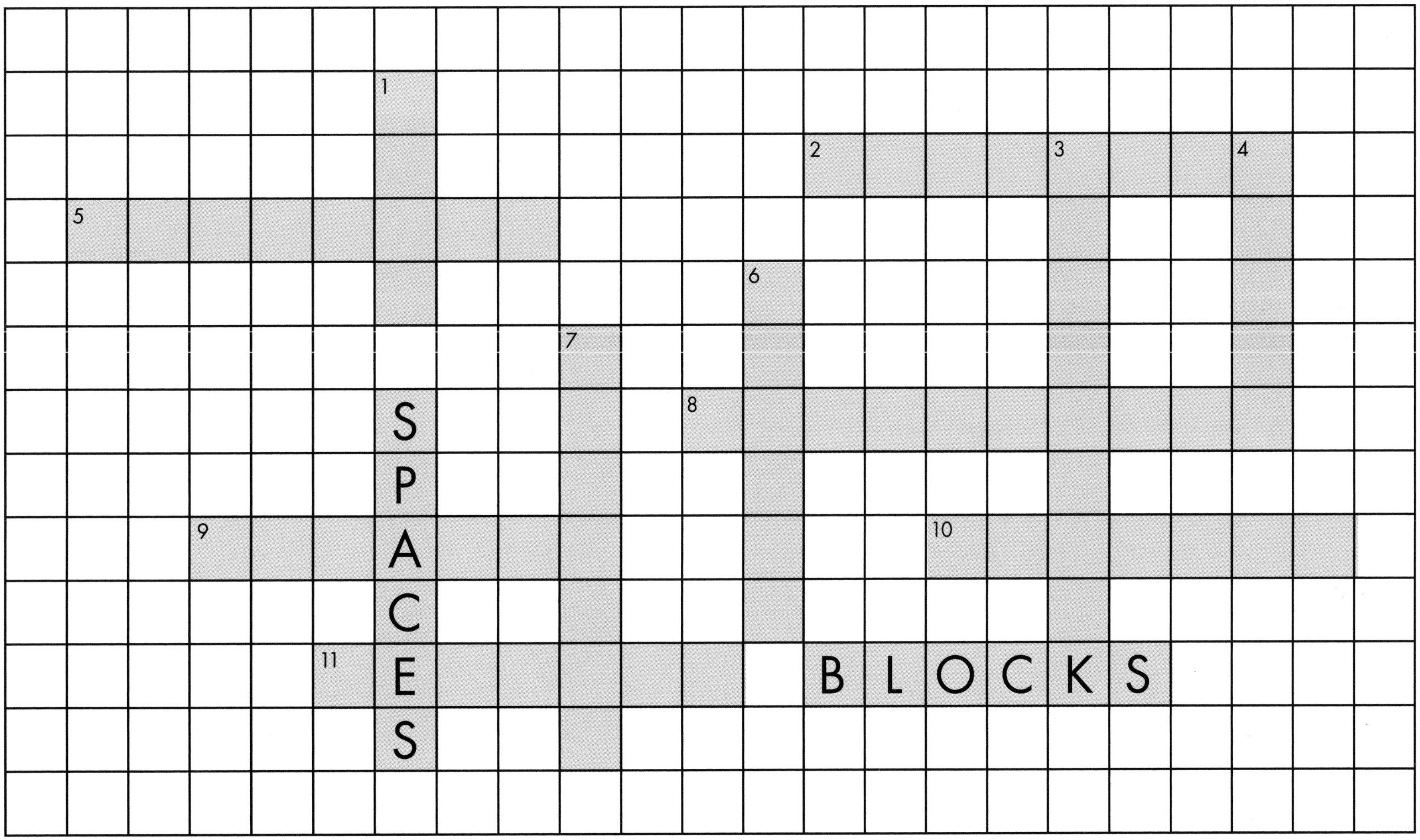
SPACES
BLOCKS

Across: 2. skylight, 5. concrete, 8. cantilever, 9. veranda, 10. Froebel, 11. textile; *Down:* 1. open, 3. inglenook, 4. tower, 6. hearth, 7. organic

FRANK LLOYD WRIGHT HOUSES TO VISIT

The best way to understand what a Frank Lloyd Wright house is really like is to visit one. Many of his houses are preserved as museums for all of us to visit, learn from, and enjoy. The following list will help you find the house nearest to you. Most have websites with complete information about the house's history, tour hours, events, and more. Talk over the best way for you to visit one of these houses with your parents.

Northeastern United States

Fallingwater
www.fallingwater.org
PO Box R, Mill Run, PA 15464
(412) 329-8501
Built for the Kaufmann family in 1936, Fallingwater cantilevers over the waterfall on Bear Run. Tickets for tours are available online.

Isadore and Lucille Zimmerman House
www.currier.org/collections
/zimmerman-house
192 Orange Street,
Manchester, NH 03104
(603) 669-6144
This house was built in 1950 and combines Wright's Prairie and Usonian styles. Check website for tour information—tour reservations are necessary.

Southern United States

Pope-Leighey House
www.woodlawnpopeleighey.org
PO Box 37, Mount Vernon, VA 22121
(703) 780-4000
An early Usonian-style house built in 1940. Check website for hours of tour operation.

Midwestern United States

Frank Lloyd Wright Home and Studio
http://gowright.org/home-and
-studio.html
951 Chicago Avenue, Oak Park, IL 60302
(708) 848-1500
Wright's first home and studio was built between 1889 and 1898. Daily tours are available year-round. Check website for special events.

Fabyan Villa and Japanese Garden
www.ppfv.org/fabyan.htm
Fabyan West Forest Preserve
Entrance off Route 31 (Batavia Avenue),
Geneva, IL 60174
(630) 377-6424
Check for hours of operation.

Meyer May House
http://meyermayhouse.steelcase.com
450 Madison Southeast,
Grand Rapids, MI 49503
(616) 246-4821
This brick prairie house was built in 1908. Check website for tour times.

Seth Peterson Cottage
www.sethpeterson.org
400 Viking Drive, Reedsburg, WI 53959
The cottage is available for rent and offers kids an excellent opportunity to sleep in a Frank Lloyd Wright house. Check website for availability.

Taliesin

www.taliesinpreservation.org
Route 3, Spring Green, WI 53588
(608) 588-2511
Built between 1902 and 1925, this group of buildings was Wright's home and studio. Open May 1 through October 31. Check ahead for tour availability and reservations.

Frederick C. Robie House

www.gowright.org/research/wright-robie
-house.html
5757 South Woodlawn Avenue,
Chicago, IL 60637
(312) 702-8374
The finest of the prairie houses, the Robie House was built in 1908. Advance tickets are highly recommended.

James Charnley House

www.sah.org/about-sah/
charnley-persky-house
1365 North Astor Street, Chicago, IL 60610
(312) 951-8006
Wright designed this small townhouse in 1891 while he was working as a draftsman. Tours are limited. Check ahead for schedule.

Dana-Thomas House

www.dana-thomas.org
301 East Lawrence Avenue,
Springfield, IL 62703
(217) 782-6776
Built in 1900, this is the largest of Wright's prairie houses and is a National Historic Landmark. Check online for hours of operation.

Lowell Walter House

www.iowadnr.gov/Destinations/StateParks
RecAreas/IowasStateParks/ParkDetails
.aspx?ParkID=3
PO Box 1, Quasquenton, IA 52362
(319) 934-3572
Built on a bluff above the Wapispinicon River, this is a large group of buildings. Check ahead for tour times.

Southwestern United States

Taliesin West

www.franklloydwright.org/about
/TaliesinWestTours.html
Cactus Road and 108th Street,
Scottsdale, AZ 85261
(602) 860-2700
This was Wright's winter home and studio. It is now the home of the Frank Lloyd Wright School of Architecture. Check the online Tour Calendar for tour times and availability.

Hollyhock House

http://hollyhockhouse.net
4808 Hollywood Boulevard, Barnsdall Park,
Los Angeles, CA 90027
(213) 662-7272 or (213) 485-4581
A 1918 house set on a hilltop. Check ahead to see if restoration is complete and house is open for touring.

Ennis-Brown House

http://ennishouse.com
2655 Glendower Avenue,
Los Angeles, CA 90027
(213) 660-0607
A textile block house built in 1923–24. Check ahead to see if restoration is complete and house is open for touring.

Freeman House

www.usc.edu/dept/architecture/slide
/Freeman
1962 Glencoe Way, Los Angeles, CA 90068
(213) 851-0671
A textile block house built in 1923–24. Check ahead to see if restoration is complete and house is open for touring.

NOTES

Chapter 1

"The maple-wood blocks": Wright, *Frank Lloyd Wright: A Testament.*

"adding tired to tired": Wright, *Frank Lloyd Wright: An Autobiography*, 17.

"Work is an adventure that makes": Wright, *Frank Lloyd Wright: An Autobiography*, 21.

Chapter 3

Although most of the White City: Thorne-Thomsen, *Greene & Greene for Kids*, 26.

Chapter 9

"I would hear from [Aline] when": Wright, *Frank Lloyd Wright: An Autobiography*, 227.

Chapter 10

"The Bauhaus was not an institution": Wingler, *The Bauhaus*, vii.

Chapter 11

"Why don't you write to Mr. Wright?": E-mail correspondence with Jim Berger, July 3, 2013.

Chapter 12

"When the sky at Taliesin was dark": Pfeiffer, *Frank Lloyd Wright: The Masterworks*, 176.

"We must study nature": Forsee, *Frank Lloyd Wright: Rebel in Concrete*, 11.

"Geometric Shape Cookies": Thorne-Thomsen, *Why the Cake Won't Rise*, 139.

GLOSSARY

abstract Art that uses only lines, colors, and geometric shapes. The objects in an abstract painting do not look the way they do in real life.

balcony A platform that sticks out from a building. Balconies are surrounded by railings for safety.

cantilever A free horizontal piece, such as a tree branch, that protrudes from a support, such as a tree trunk.

Chicago School A style of architecture that was developed by several Chicago architects in the late 1800s.

classical style A style inspired by the architecture of ancient Greece and Rome.

draftsman or draftswoman A person who draws plans and designs for buildings.

druid priests Singing storytellers who were the religious men of the ancient Celts who lived in the British Isles.

1893 Chicago World's Fair A fair in which countries from all around the world built pavilions on a special fairground in Chicago. The countries displayed their latest accomplishments in science and manufacturing. Also known as the White City.

freestanding wall A wall that is not attached to anything at the top.

geometry The branch of mathematics that studies shapes in space. Geometry that deals with two-dimensional figures drawn on a flat surface is plane geometry. Geometry that deals with three-dimensional figures that have length, width, and thickness is solid geometry.

"gingerbread" The fancy cutout decorations used on Victorian-style houses.

hearth The part of the floor where a fire is made. When the hearth is in a building, the structure above it is called a fireplace.

hexagon A polygon with six sides.

inglenook A corner place where you can sit next to a fireplace.

insulation A material that prevents the movement of heat.

organic An approach to architecture and design inspired by the harmony of shapes, colors, and patterns found in nature.

polygon A plane geometry shape, such as a square, formed by straight lines called sides.

porch A part of a building that is open to the outside and usually covered with a roof.

polyhedron A shape from solid geometry that has many sides, which are polygons. A cube is an example of a polyhedron; the sides of a cube are squares.

prairie Patches of level or slightly hilly land covered with wild grasses and very few trees.

realistic Describes objects in art that look the same way they do in real life. The people and things in a realistic painting look the way they do in real life.

symbols Pictures that stand for words.

symmetry A similar size, shape, and pattern of shapes on either side of a straight line.

tabletop mesa A land formation with a flat top that is surrounded by steep rock walls on all sides. Tabletop mesas are common in the southwestern United States.

terrace A paved area that surrounds a house and is open to the sky; it is usually surrounded by gardens.

tower A building or part of a building that is much higher than it is wide. Towers are often attached to Victorian buildings. When a tower rises to a height greater than the roof of a house, it makes a good lookout place.

turret A small, usually round tower that is attached to a building's corner and has a winding staircase inside. Turrets were used as lookouts and as places from which a castle could be defended. Castles often have several turrets.

veranda A large porch attached to a house and covered with a roof.

BIBLIOGRAPHY

Barney, Maginel Wright. *The Valley of the God-Almighty Joneses: Reminiscences of Frank Lloyd Wright's Sister*. New York: Appleton-Century, 1965.

Blumenson, John. *Identifying American Architecture: A Pictorial Guide to Styles and Terms, 1600–1945*. New York: W. W. Norton & Co., 1981.

Connors, Joseph. *The Robie House of Frank Lloyd Wright*. Chicago: The University of Chicago Press, 1984.

Costantino, Maria. *Frank Lloyd Wright*. New York: Crescent Books, 1991.

Forsee, Aylesa. *Frank Lloyd Wright: Rebel in Concrete*. Philadelphia: Macrae Smith Company, 1959.

Forsee, Aylesa. *Men of Modern Architecture*. Philadelphia: Macrae Smith Company, 1966.

Gebhard, David. *Romanza: The California Architecture of Frank Lloyd Wright*. San Francisco: Chronicle Books, 1988.

Historic American Buildings Survey. *What Style Is It?: A Guide to American Architecture*. Washington, DC: The Preservation Press, 1983.

Hoffman, Donald. *Frank Lloyd Wright's Fallingwater: The House and Its History*. New York: Dover Publications, Inc. 1978.

Hoffman, Donald. *Frank Lloyd Wright's Robie House: The Illustrated Story of an Architectural Masterpiece*. New York: Dover Publications, Inc., 1984.

House Beautiful. June 1992, page 46.

Larkin, David and Bruce Brooks Pfeiffer. *Frank Lloyd Wright the Masterpieces*. New York: Rizzoli International Publications, Inc. 1993.

Kenneway, Eric. *Origami: Paperfolding for Fun*. London: Octopus Books, Ltd., 1980.

Murphy, Wendy Bueher. *Frank Lloyd Wright, Genius! The Artist and the Process*. Englewood Cliffs, NJ: Silver Burdett Press, 1990.

Naden, Corinne J. *Frank Lloyd Wright: The Rebel Architect*. New York: Franklin Watts, Inc., 1968.

Ravielli, Anthony. *An Adventure in Geometry*. New York: Viking Press, 1957.

Russel, Solveig Paulsen. *Lines and Shapes: A First Look at Geometry*. New York: Henry Z. Walck, Inc., 1965.

Sergeant, John. *Frank Lloyd Wright's Usonian Houses*. New York: Whitney Library of Design, Watson-Guptill Publications, 1984.

Sitomer, Mindel and Harry. *What Is Symmetry?* New York: Thomas Y. Crowell Company, 1970.

Smithsonian Magazine. "The Triumph of Frank Lloyd Wright," June 2009.

Thorne-Thomsen, Kathleen. *Greene & Greene for Kids*. Salt Lake City: Gibbs Smith, Publisher, 2004.

Thorne-Thomsen, Kathleen (with Linda Brownridge). *Why the Cake Won't Rise and the Jelly Won't Set*. New York: A & W Publishers, Inc., 1979.

Vakahama, Voshie. *The Joy of Origami*. Tokyo: Shufunotono/Japan Publications, 1985.

Willard, Charlotte. *Frank Lloyd Wright: American Architect*. New York: The Macmillan Company, 1972.

Wingler, Hans M. *The Bauhaus*. Cambridge, London: The MIT Press, 1969.

Wright, Frank Lloyd. *An Autobiography*. New York: Duell, Sloan and Pearce, 1943.

Wright, Frank Lloyd. *Frank Lloyd Wright: A Testament*. New York: Horizon Press, 1957.

Wright, John Lloyd. *My Father, Frank Lloyd Wright*. New York: Dover Publications, Inc., 1992.

INDEX

Page numbers in *italics* refer to pictures.

abstract drawings (activity), 71–72
Adler & Sullivan, 14
air conditioning, 42
All Souls Church, 12
Annunciation Greek Orthodox Church,
  105–*106*
arches, 40
architectural plans (activity), 55–57
architectural styles
  Arts and Crafts, vii, *22*
  Bauhaus School, 78, 80
  Beaux Arts, 15, 18, 19, 38, 66
  Chicago School, 7, 9, 38
  Colonial, *65*, 99
  comparisons (activity), 64–66
  Craftsman, *65*
  English, *65*
  Frank Lloyd Wright, vii
  Modern, 66, 80
  Prairie, vii, 37–41, 66
  Queen Anne Victorian, *64*
  Richardsonian Romanesque style,
    18, *40*
  Shingle, vii, *22*
  Spanish, *65*
  Storybook, 66
  Textile Block, 70

Usonian, 89
Victorian, 21–*22*, *64*
Arts and Crafts style, vii, *22*
attics, *38–39*
Auditorium Building, 9
Avery Coonley House, 41, 48

Barnsdall, Aline, 67–68
Barnsdall, Sugar Top, 68–69, *70*
basements, 38–39, 89, 96
Bauhaus School, 78, 80
bean plants (activity), 4–5
Bear Run, 84
Beaux Arts style, 15, 18, 19, 38, 66
Berger, Jim, 96–97
Berger family, 96
Bogk House, *76–77*
Broadacre City, 79, 84
building materials
  concrete, 42, 68–70, 104
  natural appearance, 22, *39*, *53*, *61*, *85*,
    102
  steel framing, 7, 9, 69
Burnham, Daniel, vii, 7, 9, 19, 37, 38
buttercream frosting (recipe), 115

cantilevers (activity), 86–87
Centennial International Exhibition,
  1–2

Cheney, Edwin, 40, 60
Cheney, Martha "Mamah," 40, 59–61
Cheney House, 40–*41*
Chicago, Illinois, 7–8, 15, 19, 24, 38, 51,
  61, 80
Chicago School, 7, 9, 38
Chicago Stock Exchange Building, 9
Chicago World's Fair, 15, 19
Christmas celebrations, 30, 33, *33*
cinnamon muffins (recipe), 110
city design (activity), 81–83
city life, 78
Colonial style, *65*
colors, *39*, *53*, *62*
concrete, 42, 68–70, 104
cookies, geometric shape (recipe), 114
cooking (activity), 44
Coonley House, 41, 48
Corwin, Cecil, 13, 24
Craftsman Bungalow, *65*
crossword puzzles (activity), 116–117

Dana House, 41
dining room (Wright Home), 29–*30*
doghouses, 96–97
doors, hidden, *53*, 55
drawings, abstract (activity), 71–72
drawings, architectural (activity),
  55–57

Easter celebrations, *33, 105–106*
École des Beaux Arts, 15, 18
Edward (dog), *96–97*
elements of nature, 61, 68, 85, 88
elevation drawings, *57*
English style, *65*

Fabyan, George, 43
Fabyan Villa, *43*
Fallingwater, *84–85*
festivals (activities), *108–115*
Fir Tree House, *100–101*
Flatiron Building, *38*
floor plans, *55–57*
Frank Lloyd Wright Home, *21–23,
29–31*
Frank Lloyd Wright Studio, *24–25*
Frederick C. Robie House, *50–56*
Froebel, Friedrich, 2
Froebel Gifts, 2, 6, 10
front doors, *53, 55*
funeral, *107*

geometric shape cookies (recipe), 114
geometric shapes (activity), *10–11*
Germany, 80
gingerbread houses, 21
graham cracker models (activity), *86–87*
Great Depression, 78

Gropius, Walter, 80
Guggenheim, Solomon R., 103
Guggenheim Museum, *103–104, 105*

Hagia Sophia, 105
Hanna, Jean, 90
Hanna, Paul, 90
Hannah "Honeycomb" House, *90–91*
Heurtley, Arthur, 39
Heurtley, Grace, 39
Heurtley House, *36, 39–40*
hexagonal designs (activity), *92–93*
Hinzenberg, Olgivanna Lazovich,
77–78
historical houses (activity), 98–99
Hollyhock House, *68–70*
Home Insurance Building, 7, 9
Honeycomb House, *90–91*
Hubbard, Elbert, 42

illustration (activity), 26–27
Imperial Hotel, 68
inglenook, 22, *23*
Institute of Design, 80

Jacobs, Herbert, 89
Jacobs, Katherine, 89
Jacobs Usonian House, *89–90*
Japan, 45, 68

Japanese kites (activity), 45–47
Jeanneret, Charles-Édouard, 80
Jenney, William Le Baron, vii, 7, 9, 38
Johnson's Wax building, 101, *102*

Kaufmann, Edgar, Jr., 84, 85
Kaufmann House, *84–85*
kites (activity), 45–47

Larkin, John D., 42
Larkin Building, *41–42*
Larkin Company, 41–42
Le Corbusier, 80
Lloyd Jones, Anna (later, Wright), 1–2, 6
Lloyd Jones, Jenkin, 12, 42
Lloyd Jones family, 2–3, 42

Macdonald, George, 108–109
Merchants National Bank Building,
14, 17
Midway Gardens, *61*
milk with honey, warm (recipe), 115
Modern style, *66*
money-saving techniques, 89–90
Montauk Block building, *9*
Morris, William, 14
motorcars, 51
murders, 61
Museum of Modern Art, 78

nature, as inspiration, 3, 14, 21–22, 53, 70, 84–85, 90, 96, 103, 106. *see also* organic architecture
New Bauhaus, 80
Noel, Miriam, 77

Oak Park, Illinois, 21, 23, 24, 30, 41, 42–43
Oak Park Unitarian Church, 42–43
oatmeal (activity), 44
Ocatillo camp, 78, 89
office buildings, 41–42
Olive Hill, 67, 69
Olmstead, Frederick Law, 19
orange spice iced tea (recipe), 111
organic architecture, 14, 21–22, 33, 37–38, 52, 59, 78, 85
origami (activity), 34–35

paper dyeing (activity), 62–63
paper folding (activity), 34–35
Peters, Brandock, *102*
Peterson, Seth, 95–96
Peterson Cottage, *94–96*
plans (activity), 55–57
planters, *24*, 53
plant growth (activity), 4–5
plan views, 81
playrooms, 30–*31*, 41, 54, 68–69
polygons, 10–11

polyhedrons, 10–11
prairie houses, 37–41, 51–52, 54
Prairie style, *66*

Queen Anne Victorian, *64*

radiant heat, 89, 97
ranch-style houses, 90
relief sculpture (activity), 73–75
restoration research (activity), 98–99
Richardson, Henry Hobson, vii, 14, 15, 18, 40
Richardsonian Romanesque style, *40*
Robie, Frederick C., 51, *52*
Robie, Frederick, Jr., *54*
Robie, Lora, 51
Robie House, *50–56*
Root, John Wellborn, 9, 38

San Marcos hotel, 77–78
Seth Peterson Cottage, *94–96*
shapes (activity), 26–27
Shaughnessy (dog), 97
Shingle style, 22
Silsbee, J. L., 12, 13
skyscrapers, 9, 77
"So Long, Frank Lloyd Wright" (Simon), vii
Space Race, 107
Spanish style, *65*

spiral shapes, 103–104
spring festival (activity), 108–111
stained glass design (activity), 48–49
stained glass windows, *39*, 41, 68, *53*, 104
steel framing, 7, 9, 69
Storybook style, *66*
studio office, 24–*25*
Sullivan, Louis, vii, 7, 13, 14–*15*, 21, 23, 40
Susan Lawrence Dana House, 41
symmetry (activity), 16–17

Taliesin, *58*, 61
Taliesin Fellowship, 78–*79*, 105
Taliesin Palette, 62
Taliesin West, 89, 105
Textile Block houses, 70
textile blocks (activity), 73–75
Tobin, Catherine (later, Wright), *20*
Transportation Building, *40*
Trinity Church, *18*, 40

Unity Temple, 42–*43*
Usonian houses, 89–90

van der Rohe, Ludwig Mies, vii, 78, 80
Victorian style, 21–*22*, 40, 64

Ward Willits House, 41
water sounds (activity), 88

White City, *19*, 38

Willits House, 41

window design (activity), 48–49

Winslow, William, 24

Winslow House, *24*

winter festival (activity), 112–115

Wisconsin (map), 12

Wisconsin state capitol building, 6

women's suffrage, 60

Wright, Anna Lloyd Jones (mother), 1–2, *23*

Wright, Catherine Lloyd (daughter), 30, *32*

Wright, Catherine Tobin (wife)
    family life, 22, 29–33, 60
    marriage, 20, 77

pictured, *20, 23, 28, 32*

Wright, David (son), 29, 30, *32*

Wright, Frances (daughter), 29, 30, *32*

Wright, Frank Lloyd
    childhood, 1–3
    death, 106–107
    education, 6
    family life, 22, 29–33, 59–60, 77
    legacy, vii, 106
    Mamah Cheney and, 59–61
    marriages, 20, 77
    personality, 33
    pictured, *2, 3, 12, 20, 23, 78, 102*
    as a teacher, 78

    travels, 45, 68
    Welsh heritage, 61

Wright, Iovanna Lloyd (daughter), 77

Wright, Jane (sister), 2

Wright, John (son), 30, *32*

Wright, Lloyd (son), *23*, 30, *32*

Wright, Maginel (sister), 2, *23*, 26, 33

Wright, Miriam Noel (wife), 77

Wright, Olgivanna Lloyd (wife), 77–78

Wright, Robert Llewellyn (son), 29, 30, *32*

Wright, William Carey (father), 1, 2, 3

Wright Home and Studio, 21–*23*, *24–25,*
  29–31

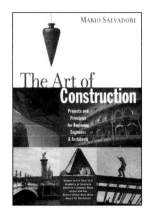

$16.95 (CAN $18.95)

978-1-55652-080-8

*Also available in
e-book formats*

The Art of Construction
Projects and Principles for Beginning
Engineers & Architects

Mario Salvadori

"Introduces maturing minds to the principles that guide architects and engineers as they design and construct buildings and bridges." —*School Shop*

"An extraordinary book." —*Chicago Tribune*

"A top choice for serious architecture students." —*School Library Journal*

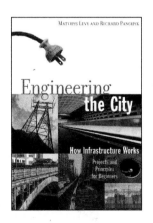

$14.95 (CAN $22.95)

978-1-55652-419-6

*Also available in
e-book formats*

Engineering the City
How Infrastructure Works

Matthys Levy and Richard Panchyk

"Future engineers, math enthusiasts, and students seeking ideas for science projects will all be fascinated by this book." —*Booklist*

"A terrific book to help you answer those tough questions about everyday structures in an urban environment . . . filled with useful drawings and pictures . . . loaded with experiments, design projects and construction diagrams." —*Demolition*

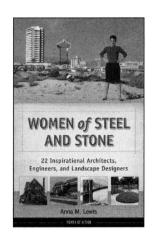

$19.95 (CAN $21.95)

978-1-61374-508-3

Also available in e-book formats

Women of Steel and Stone

22 Inspirational Architects, Engineers, and Landscape Designers

Anna M. Lewis

"What caused a few women to counter the trends and choose these professions? What difficulties did they face in fields so new to them? And did the influences that marked their early histories reveal themselves in their work and careers? Anna Lewis's book raises these questions, central for young people considering the future." —Denise Scott Brown, cofounder of Venturi, Scott Brown and Associates

"A truly inspirational read, this is the kind of book that will motivate young readers to learn more about a field they may not have thought about much before." —*VOYA*

"A much-needed, clearly presented history." —*School Library Journal*

"Anna Lewis skillfully delivers real-life stories of successful women in these fields to inspire and inform readers." —Lucy Sanders, CEO and cofounder of the National Center for Women and Information Technology (NCWIT)

Available at your favorite bookstore, by calling (800) 888-4741, or at www.chicagoreviewpress.com

CHICAGO REVIEW PRESS